TAKEN
CAPTIVE

TAKEN CAPTIVE

The secret to capturing your piece of America's
multi-billion dollar insurance industry

R. WESLEY SIERK, III

RMA PRESS
LOS ANGELES, CALIFORNIA

Published by RMA Press

Printed in the United States of America

This publication is designed to provide accurate and authoritative in-formation to the reader regarding the subjects addressed within. The information within is not intended to provide guidance to any specific set of circumstances. Readers are advised to seek guidance from qualified professionals regarding their specific situations and to not rely exclusively on the information, guidance or advice provided within this material.

Library of Congress Cataloging-in-Publication Data:

Sierk, R. Wesley
Taken Captive / R. Wesley Sierk
Includes bibliographical references
ISBN 978-0-9801925-0-6   0-9801925-0-6
1. Insurance. 2. Taxation—Small Business 3. Small
Business Financial Planning. 4. Wealth Management.
I. Title.

Acknowledgements

There are so many people who support me on a day-to-day basis. I would divide them into personal and professional, but being a business owner, it is very hard to separate the personal from the professional.

Personally, I owe a huge debt of gratitude to my wife. Leslie and I have been together since I started in the insurance business and she always believed in me even when I lost faith in myself. She is my best friend, and the best mother in the world. You have the patience of Job, and I can not say Thank You enough. You give me the strength and inspiration to do what I do everyday. I love you.

When I read books, most people always thank their parents. I often wonder whether people thank their parents because they ought to or they feel they should. I can say without reservation I have two of the finest parents that have walked the earth. They have a strong marriage and have taught us children how to love and cherish each other. My mother raised 4 kids (all within 2 years of age). We have just one son, and that can be challenging. I can not fathom how she managed to raise us all and always have a smile on her face. I would like to thank my father Rick. Everyone that has met my father agrees he is one of the finest people they have ever met. He is smart, honest, and one of the hardest working people I have met. My two best characteristics I learned from him: work ethic, and intellectual curiosity. Without those two things I would not have risen to the point in my career I currently find myself. In addition to the guidance he has given me, he spent countless hours, often at the beginning or end of his 12 hour work day, to help me with editing the book. Thank You.

I also have to thank my partners and friends Jarid Beck and Max Jong. Jarid and I have worked together daily for the last 5 years. He has developed into one of the best business people and a true student of the insurance business. I could not travel, keep my speaking engagements, and sales appointments without him there to keep the business running and focused. He wears two hats and is great at both. On the one side, he interfaces daily with the clients on the technical aspects of all the plans we have implemented. This often entails coordinating 4 or 5 separate service providers to get thing done. One the other side he runs the operation of the business. He is the COO, and we are all lucky to have him. No ball gets dropped and we are free to focus on what we do best, create.

My other partner and longtime friend is Max Jong. Words cannot express how much it means to be in business with one of the people you respect most in the world. If I could choose anyone to be in business with, your name would always be at the top of my list. Your professionalism and integrity goes unmatched in an industry that is always plagued with half truths and secrecy. Thank you for taking the leap of faith a few years ago, joining Jarid and myself, and helping to create this company. One of my business philosophies is: you never get extraordinary results from ordinary people. You always get ordinary results from ordinary people.

I would also need to thank Erin Shepard. I still remember the first day I interviewed her. I could see so much promise in her. She has not let us down and has grown personally and professionally and has become one of my "go to" people. I know when I give her something to do, it just gets done. We have a great friendship as well as a working relationship. I look forward to years of great work ahead.

One of the newest members of our team is Sasha Gonzales. We "inherited" Sasha when Max joined our practice. She is bright, articulate, and a pleasure to have as a part of our company.

No thank you list would be complete without the person who keeps my world running and organized on a daily basis, Rachel Downen. She is one of the most extraordinary people I have ever met. I often get criticized for surrounding myself with friends. She and I had been great friends for years before we worked together and if I had taken people's advice and not hired her for that reason, I would have lost out on so much. As a result of working together, I am a better person. You make it a joy to come to work. For all you do, I can never say thank you enough.

Professionally there have been so many that have helped me formulate my vision of insurance. I could not thank them all by name or the book would be filled. I thank everyone from my earliest days at Northwestern Mutual under the supervision of Bob Kerrigan and Shawn Mackey to my current interactions with insurance commissioners and regulators. We are blessed in California to have an insurance commissioner like Steve Poizner. He is doing the right thing, for the right reasons. This book is written to explore captive insurance and many of the regulators have been so extremely helpful and forth coming with valuable insight. This is a non-domicile specific book, but I would like to thank and commend Utah's insurance Commissioner Kent Michie on his selection of Don Spann and Eric Showgren as the captive regulators for his state. Although the relationship is new, these are two of the best and brightest in the entire captive world.

Lastly, I would like to thank the man instrumental in helping me write, organize, and complete this book, Bob Layne. He is a master at his craft and a true professional in every sense of the word. Bob has great vision and a great support staff surrounding him. When I think of Bob, I think of the following poem by Myra Brooks Welch:

"The Touch of the Master's Hand"

It was battered and scarred,
And the auctioneer thought it
Hardly worth his while
To waste his time on the old violin,
But he held it up with a smile.
"What am I bid, good people," he cried,
"Who starts the bidding for me?"
"One dollar, one dollar, Do I hear two?"
"Two dollars, who makes it three?"
"Three dollars once, three dollars twice, going for three,"

But, No,
From the room far back a grey haired man
Came forward and picked up the bow,
Then wiping the dust from the old violin
And tightening up the strings,
He played a melody, pure and sweet,
As sweet as the angel sings.

The music ceased and the auctioneer
With a voice that was quiet and low,
Said "What now am I bid for this old violin?"
As he held it aloft with its bow.
"One thousand, one thousand, Do I hear two?"
"Two thousand, Who makes it three?"
"Three thousand once, three thousand twice,
Going and gone," said he.

The audience cheered,
But some of them cried,
"We just don't understand."
"What changed its worth?"
Swift came the reply.
"The Touch of the Master's Hand."

In many ways I feel you took the earliest ideas and manuscripts that were much like that old violin, and played a beautiful melody. Bob, my book is better because it was touched by the master's hand. Thank You.

Contents

Introduction

**"The difficulty lies not so much in developing
new ideas as in escaping from old ones."**
John Maynard Keyes

Inspiration comes in many forms. The inspiration for this book came during my search for resources to share with my clients. My goal was to identify relevant, intellectually sound, easy-to-read material that would help educate my clients on the purpose and value of insurance in general and captive insurance companies specifically. I started with books on insurance and how it operates as an industry. What I found were esoteric encyclopedias useless in describing how my client could and should buy insurance.

Also useless in helping me achieve my goal, was the information contained in what seemed like thousands of insurance books lining the shelves of bookstores, libraries, and the brokers' shelves. My search also took me to the volumes of articles published by Business Week, the Wall Street Journal, Barron's, and countless other mainstream financial journals offering advice to their readers about what kind and how to purchase insurance.

But where were the resources for the very wealthy and sophisticated investors: the entrepreneurs and CEOs, the architects, real estate developers and builders, the professional athletes and entertainers, the hedge-fund managers and venture capitalists? They are in a different situation and should be purchasing their insurance a different way. In fact, my firm's work has long demonstrated that in many cases, it is these types of professionals who should do more than *purchase* insurance, rather they should *own* their own insurance company, a captive insurance company. And as I searched for that resource that would help in communicating the value of this strategy, I came up empty—except for the simple idea that perhaps it was time to write my own.

It is my belief the insurance industry is broken and successful business people should take advantage of the federal laws that allow them to escape the hard and soft market cycles of traditional insurance and start their own insurance companies. I have been in the insurance industry for over 15 years and am continually astonished at what I see happening in the insurance marketplace.

What is the state of the current insurance industry?
The insurance industry is challenged in many ways. It is an industry plagued with inefficiencies that is costing businesses hundreds of millions in excess premiums. Businesses pay insurance premiums that increase at double digit rates year after year. Many of these businesses have very little claims and when faced with a situation where they need insurance, the claims are often denied. I would like to say this is a new phenomenon, but it is not. This seems to be the status quo.

Much of this has to do with the design of the policies themselves. When I present at conferences, I like to use the simple analogy of a funnel; at the top—the widest part—we have the initial language of the standard "insuring agreement." The insuring agreement is the statement that explains the type of insurance one is purchasing and how the insurance company will pay claims against the policy. It usually begins with language something like: "we will pay on your behalf...." We are at the widest part of our insurance coverage funnel; if we have a claim the insurance company will pay—sounds great!

But then as we continue to read, we begin to see "endorsements" and "exclusions" that reduce coverage and limit the insurance company's liability, and we find ourselves sliding down the funnel. Our coverage narrows.

The more we read, the narrower the funnel gets. The funnel shrinks even smaller when the insurance company imposes such conditions on the policyholder as: "the insured must notify the company in writing within 10 days of an insured loss."

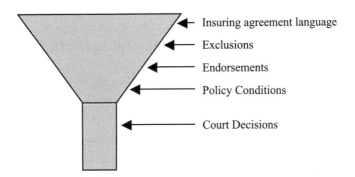

Visually where the funnel straightens out is what I refer to as public policy decisions. The insurance companies with the help of lobbyist and teams of attorneys have been highly successful in getting court decisions in their favor. Insurance companies see what arguments are successful and write contracts that take these decisions into account. This has the effect of further limiting the likelihood the insurance companies will have to pay out a claim later on a policy. As I am writing this, I opened up a binder on my desk with a policy we were retained to review for a client. I opened to the exclusion section on their Errors and Omissions policy to prove a point for this section. It read:

4. Exclusions
This policy does not cover any claim:
  (a) rising out of or resulting, directly or indirectly, from any dishonest, fraudulent, criminal, or malicious act,

error or omission, or any unintentional or knowing violation of the law, or gaining of any profit or advantage
to which the insured is not legally entitled;

Keep in mind this is an Errors and Omissions policy and in the
first line, errors and omissions are EXCLUDED. This type of
wording continued for another 7 pages. Many of the paragraphs
had to be read three or four times to follow the carrier's logic.

If this is the norm, why hasn't the industry been forced to
change? The simple answer is it doesn't have to. It has existed
for years in secrecy and has very little, if any oversight by the
federal government. The rules of the game have been tilted in
favor of the insurance companies and that is very hard to sway.
Working in the insurance industry, you would have thought El-
liot Spitzer's testimony to the U.S. Senate in November 2004
was full of deliberate mistruths. I believe Mr. Spitzer may be
the first government official that got it right. I have included a
copy of his testimony in one of the Appendices of this book
and I would urge you to read it. I hope it will be as eye-open-
ing and riveting a read for you as it was for me when I first
read it.

The purpose of the book is not to disparage the insurance industry. In fact, I am a firm believer in the value that an insurance company can offer to business. We own a few insurance
companies on our own and use the laws we are discussing to
our own business advantage. Though it may come as a surprise,
I do not believe an insurance company's highest obligation is
to the consumer. In my opinion, its obligation is to the shareholders of the company that it supports. The stockholders are
the ones who invest in the business and deserve a fair return for
the capital they invest. The only way to achieve a fair return to
the shareholders *and* give the consumers a better product at a
lower price would be to reduce the inefficiencies in the market.

This book does not spend time dissecting the industry because effecting meaningful change will take years and most likely federal intervention. The insurance industry is unique for its size and tenure in that its regulation is subject to state, not federal regulation. The insurance companies are regulated by a patchwork of laws which often conflict and confuse reason without apology. Given the industry's financial and public policy position, the state insurance commissioners are some of the most powerful people that exist in our economy. They have the ability to make or break business profitability with the stroke of a pen. And although these state insurance departments are established by the state, most are independent from the operation of the state government. They are usually run by a commissioner (either elected or appointed) who has complete control. The executive, judicial and legislative branches of that department are under the control and direction of a single individual. These insurance departments write the law, interpret the law and have their own police force and investigators to enforce the laws.

Of the many industries that are crucial to the economic well being of the United States, I rank insurance at the top of the list. After all, with the level of income, capital, and surpluses in the coffers of insurance companies, they have become the invisible banks in our economy.

As a business owner it would be comforting to know that in the traditional insurance marketplace you have a fighting chance. But I do not feel you do. Business owners often rely on others to advise them on the policies they should be purchasing. The people they often turn to have no skin in the game. Many times they are relying on the broker to bring back quotes for coverage. Although I have met hundreds of great brokers in my career, the majority are vastly overpaid and under skilled. The insurance industry and agents have done themselves a great injustice over the years by allowing insurance to become a commodity. Many of the brokers do not understand the insurance they are selling, the terms, exclusions, and policy conditions the client will be forced to adhere to in order to get a claim paid. Their attention is often far too focused on one parameter: cost.

Many business owners realize they do not have the time to learn all of the subtle nuances of policy design. They often rely on professionals other than brokers. Many of the companies we work with for example have a risk management department, or at least an individual they can point to and say, "this is our insurance expert." Often those individuals are given the task of securing quotes and sifting through them to decide what product to buy. The biggest problem with this strategy is that the decision maker for the insurance has at best a distant vested interest in the success or failure of the insurance program. Here's an example to illustrate the point.

Recently I met with the CEO of a large construction company, his CFO, and the company's risk manager. We were discussing the workers compensation program for the business. The business pays a little over $1,000,000 per year in workers compensation and the average annual losses have been in the $25,000 to $50,000 range. The business owner had not taken the time to review the losses or insurance polices in years. When the business owner looked at this, his first question was, "why aren't we self-insuring part of the workers compensation?" Very astute observation, and a painful one given that the program had not been reviewed in 10 years. Why? The business owner knew insurance was expensive, so when the rates went up year after year, he got into the habit of simply expecting it and accepting it. The business owner ultimately pays the price of insurance. If premiums rise or fall 10%, the person who feels it in loss or profit first is the business owner. It's also the business owner who must absorb rate increases in health insurance. When those rates rise by 25% over 3 years (as they did in California), the business owners can't just raise prices by 25% to keep in step with those increases. That ultimately eats into the profit of the owner.

Since the inception of captives, both federal and state legislation has been adopted and amended addressing the types of captives that are allowed, the insurance coverages they can provide, and the companies or associations permitted to create captives. Upon passage of the Federal Risk Retention Act in the early 1980s, the number of captive insurers approved substantially increased, as did the global expansion in jurisdictions that permit Captives to be domiciled within their borders. Today, nearly 6,000 captives operate globally, underwriting $300 billion in risk each year, earning annual premiums in excess of $50 billion dollars, and holding capital and surplus worth more than $60 billion.

The exponential growth in the number of captives in existence can be attributed to two major factors: 1) the difficulty of obtaining needed coverage, and 2) the volatility in prices for available coverages. When prices rise or coverage is simply difficult to obtain, companies look for alternatives that allow them protection at reasonable rates. This demand has created a substantial increase in non-admitted, surplus lines insurers issuing policies to American businesses.

In the most recent 10 years, there have been close to 500 domestic insurance company failures. These failures cost consumers in excess of $10 billion. With so many failures, it would be easy to draw the conclusion that the industry must not be very profitable. However, most of these failures were caused by gross mismanagement, not because the companies wrote bad risk. If anything, insurance companies are given more rope on which to hang themselves than is the case for companies in other industries. When they do fail, the victims are the consumers who purchased policies at a time when they believed the insurance company had adequate financial strength to qualify to write insurance. The other victims are the financially strong insurance companies who must pay into the state guarantee fund to help compensate for the carriers that are now in receivership.

In recent years, the state guarantee fund has been depleted to historic lows. It is estimated it will cost Louisiana more than $1 billion to clean up and bail out close to 80 defunct insurance companies that failed in the aftermath of hurricane Katrina. It is estimated the ultimate payout to consumers will be less than thirty cents on the dollar. With every carrier collapse the market becomes ever tighter. The tightening of the market causes prices to increase. A captive insurance company reduces the reliance of business on the ever shrinking pool of carriers admitted to write insurance. Captives are not eligible for the state guarantee fund, so no insurance revenue is spent to bail out captive insurers.

In addition to insurance company failures, the market is becoming increasingly more volatile from the increasing consolidation in the industry. There are fewer choices in insurance than there used to be, leading to less competition. Less competition and fewer choices of coverage lead to increased costs. When there are fewer insurers left, and they suffer a loss, policyholders are left with higher premiums.

Publicly traded insurance companies are more subject to volatility than a captive insurer. The main factor impacting the stock price of a publicly traded insurer is the rate of return to the shareholders not the value to the policy holders. In order to maintain a stable stock price, an insurer must continually raise and lower premiums to maintain a certain return to investors. All it takes for an insurance company to initiate a large increase in premiums is a combination of a loss on a block of business, increased reinsurance rates (even if slight), and a decrease in the investment portfolio.

Captive insurers are only interested in profitability. They charge premiums commensurate with the risk; they invest conservatively and manage the portfolio of reinsurance so they will not be subject to large premium fluctuations.

In recent years I have seen a large increase in the number of "professionals" giving captive-insurance advice. This book is intended to give clear, concise, accurate information on how a captive works and when it should be used. A captive is not, let me repeat, *not* the last greatest tax deduction in America. It is a risk-financing tool that allows the right businesses to take some of the risk of their own company, and in exchange, profit from that risk. If you run your business better than your competitors, a captive is likely right for you.

This book is intended to dispel many of the misconceptions held by business owners and advisors about when a captive is appropriate and the laws surrounding the regulation of an insurance company. We will discuss in detail, what the role of all of the parties to the captive insurance company are, how they work, normal costs, and what to demand of the providers.

The final chapter of the book combines case studies and real life examples from our practice combining all of the powerful risk management, insurance transfer, asset protection, and tax benefits a captive will provide.

As you read you will find "Captive Insight" boxes offering additional information and web links to the website www.TakenCaptive.com. I encourage you to use this tool as information is regularly updated on the website. Also, I want to add a note of caution; like many things, a little information can be dangerous. As you begin exploring whether captive insurance is right for you and your business, be sure to seek competent advice from risk management advisors who have a strong and reputable track record in the captive industry. You will save significant time and headache by doing so.

Enjoy exploring the world of captive insurance and don't hesitate to contact me with your questions.

R. Wesley Sierk, III, Long Beach, California

Chapter 1: What is a captive?

A captive insurer (or "captive") is a special-purpose insurance company formed primarily to underwrite the risks of its parent or affiliated groups. It is quite similar to a traditional, commercial insurance company in that it is licensed as an insurance company, it sets insurance- premium rates for the risks it chooses to underwrite, writes policies for the risks it insures, collects premiums and pays out claims made against those policies. The biggest difference between a captive insurer and a commercial insurance company is that a captive cannot sell insurance to the general public. It can only underwrite the risks of its parent organization or related entities. Another key difference is that the regulations governing captive insurance companies are typically less onerous than those regulations governing traditional commercial carriers.

At its most basic level a "pure" captive works like this: A corporation with one or more subsidiaries sets up a captive insurance company as a wholly owned subsidiary. The captive is capitalized and domiciled in a jurisdiction with captive-enabling legislation which allows the captive to operate as a licensed insurer. The parent identifies the risks of its subsidiaries that it wants the captive to underwrite. The captive evaluates the risks, writes policies, sets premium levels and accepts premium payments. The subsidiaries then pay the captive tax-deductible premium payments and the captive, like any insurer, invests the premium payments for future claim payouts.

Like most innovations, captive insurance companies were created to solve a set of problems; in this case, risk-financing problems we didn't know we had until we started thinking about managing and financing risk. To be sure, however, we were introduced to these problems long before we began our professional careers. For most, that introduction probably came around the time we turned 16. Beaming with unfounded confidence, we burst into the house announcing that we passed our drivers' test and were officially ready for our own personal freedom. At some point soon after our little declaration of independence, one of our parents asked how we expected to pay for the insurance.

"Insurance?" we asked.

"Yes, we've added you to our auto insurance policy and we'd like you to help pay for the additional cost."

"No problem," we said thinking, *What's the big deal? How much could it be?*

If your experience was typical, then you will remember the shock as you tried to comprehend how you—let alone *any* 16-year-old—could possibly afford such a staggering amount. And if you are male and you happened to have an older sister, your shock was eclipsed only by outrage when you learned you were being charged at least 50% more for the same coverage.

"That's not fair!" you protested as you came face to face with one of the risk-financing problems captives were developed to address: insurance rates are not based on the specific risk profile of any one particular insured or the loss history of the family or group or company. They are based on the anticipated loss frequency and severity of a population that may well *not* reflect you or your experience.

Imagine the following scenario. Let's say you grew up in a family of safe drivers who rarely or maybe even never had a reason to make a claim against your auto insurance policy. Wouldn't you have preferred to pay premiums based on your actual loss history and risk profile? And, wouldn't it have been better if instead of paying your premium to an insurance company, you could have put it in a bank account that your parents opened so the premium dollars could at least earn you some interest while they sat there waiting to cover a claim that wasn't coming? Of course!

This simple example illustrates a powerful incentive captives offer their owners: the ability to sidestep the broad strokes commercial carriers use when writing rate policies. Why not simply retain the risk inside the captive and let someone else subsidize the broader risk pool's poor experience? We address this and other benefits of forming a captive in chapter 2.

A brief historical perspective
The concept of captive insurance is not new. In fact, by some accounts, the basic concept can be traced back hundreds of years to the days when ship owners would share, exchange or otherwise transfer risk with one another in situations where commercial insurance was not available. Then, in the 1870s, the first Protection and Indemnity clubs were created. Growth of the captive insurance concept was slow however, and up until the 1950s, only about 100 captives were formed.

It wasn't until the 1970s and 1980s that the captive industry saw significant growth. This growth was partly facilitated by new legislation. In the 1970s, three states —Colorado, Tennessee and Vermont—passed laws favorable to captive formation. Then in the 1980s Congress passed federal products liability legislation making it easier to operate similar-interest captives. A hard insurance market and interest rate anomalies were the other significant forces driving the dramatic growth of the 1970s and 1980s.

Hard Market

A hard market occurs when insurance premiums increase and capacity decreases. In a hard market, insurance companies are less flexible on coverages, terms and rates.

Go to www.takencaptive.com/glossary to find more definitions.

By 1995, there were just over 3,000 captives and today the number exceeds 6,000. Not surprisingly, some of the largest and most sophisticated organizations were the first to explore, develop and refine the modern captive market. In fact, more than 40% of major U.S. corporations operate at least one captive. These organizations discovered that through forming a captive, they could obtain greater flexibility and control over their risk-financing needs without relying exclusively on the traditional insurance market.

When an organization decides to establish a captive insurance company, one of the key decisions it must make is to determine where the captive will be legally domiciled. Although the organization may be familiar with establishing a subsidiary company, setting up a captive is different. As mentioned, certain jurisdictions have developed favorable legislation to attract companies interested in establishing a captive model while others have established legislation that is decidedly unfavorable.

Today, the leading offshore domiciles are Bermuda, the Cayman Islands and the British Virgin Islands. In the U.S., the leading domiciles are Vermont, Hawaii, South Carolina and Arizona. We explore the issues around evaluating and choosing a domicile in chapter 5.

Figure 1.1 - Leading captive domiciles

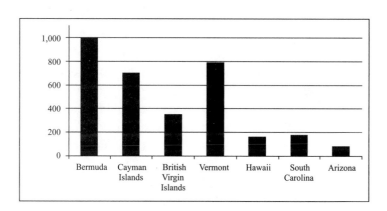

Addressing risk: captive vs. traditional market
The problems that are addressed today by captive insurance companies are problems that most organizations face in one form or another:

- unavailability of coverage
- coverage that is too expensive
- coverage that can't be tailored appropriately for an organization's needs
- premium rates that do not meet a particular organization's loss profile
- inflexible policies
- inflexible terms
- inability to estimate loss frequency or loss severity
- lack of a tax benefit for retaining risk

Like any good business venture, the companies that make up the traditional insurance market are motivated by making a profit. They are in a sense investment companies. They assess market risk, determine what risk they are willing to take based on market averages, take premium payments against those risks, invest the premium payments and ultimately they hope to pay out less in claims than they were able to earn in premium payments and investment income.

Within this business strategy, there is little room for any significant deviation from broadly established principles of acceptable levels of risk and the projected amount of premium payment required to cover those risks. This means opportunities to negotiate better-than-average market rates and opportunities to negotiate customized coverages are limited—even if the company negotiating better rates has a risk profile that is substantially better than average. In fact, insurance companies are counting on these low-risk companies to offset the risk associated with higher-risk companies who are in effect paying less than they should.

At its core, a captive insurance company is a risk-financing tool. It places more risk-management control and financial control into the hands of the owner of the captive than exists in a typical commercial insurer-insured relationship. Unlike what occurs in the traditional insurance market, the risks that are underwritten by the captive are precisely the risks that the insured needs underwritten. The policy terms are designed to meet the specific needs of the insured and the rates are based on the specific loss profile/loss experience of the insured—not the average loss rate of the market.

You can think of it in terms of buying clothing. While the traditional insurance market offers small, medium or large, a captive insurer measures a precise fit for its insured. However, unlike the choice between custom-tailored and "off the rack," a well-planned, well-structured captive strategy will most likely cost the insured *less* than the traditional commercial-insurance route. The combination of custom-tailored and less expensive is the reason captives have become so prevalent today.

How integrated are captives in today's market?
Based on the existence of more than 6,000 operating captive insurance companies and more than three decades of mainstream market and regulatory acceptance, the captive insurance model can be considered, by nearly all measures, a well-accepted risk-management option in today's market.

This was certainly not always the case. State and federal insurance regulators and tax authorities have scrutinized, analyzed and challenged from many angles the use of captives. In the end, the captive market is better for it. What stands in the market today are captive options that have been clarified and refined. The long-term value of a well-structured captive is now much more clear and predictable.

To say that the captive insurance model is well accepted does not mean that there are no longer any challenges from a regulatory perspective. It is true that there are standard captive structures that have become well accepted. But the market continues to evolve and new captive structures and innovative uses for captives are being designed all the time. As you would expect, any new business methodology that either impacts the Internal Revenue Service's standard of living or runs afoul of an insurance regulator's standards of acceptable practice will be subject to some degree of scrutiny. Nevertheless, the fact that the debate has moved from "should a captive be permitted to exist at all" to whether certain customized versions should be permitted is another strong indicator of market acceptance.

Captive Insight

Do you know the name of the major commercial insurance company that started as a captive for one of America's longest-standing retailers?

Go to www.takencaptive.com and enter the phrase: "retail captive" in the "**Captive Insight**" box for the answer.

There is no question that one of the most important drivers for market acceptance and long-term market integration of captives was the recognition in the mid 1990s that in proper circumstances, premiums paid to captives would be deductible. The IRS affirmed the deductibility of premiums paid to a captive by the captive owner's separate subsidiary companies. Premiums paid to a captive directly by the parent company exclusively were not deductible (see Figure 1.3).

Once the premium deductibility issue was settled to the point where tax professionals could be confident in premium deductibility, captives started forming in record numbers.

Figure 1.2 - Captive structure for premium deductibility

Premium Deductibility

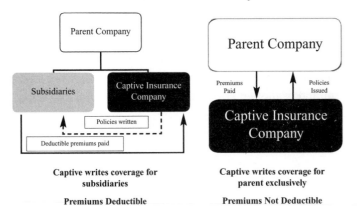

Captive writes coverage for subsidiaries

Premiums Deductible

Captive writes coverage for parent exclusively

Premiums Not Deductible

In the 15 years between 1991 and 2006, the total number of captives in the world market rose from 3,000 to 6,000 – a doubling of the number globally. During the same period, Vermont, the leading captive jurisdiction in the U.S., saw a nearly 340% increase in captives formed from 234 to 791.

One reason for the significant jump in numbers of captives is that smaller companies have discovered the captive benefits. Initially, the captive market was shaped by the largest corporations with complex risk-financing issues to manage. Once captives became commonplace, opportunities for their use became more obvious and available to smaller companies looking for flexibility and greater control. For example, captives are frequently used today by a variety of small-business professionals ranging from contractors to physicians. These professionals have discovered the distinct advantages of using a captive as a key component of their overall risk-financing strategy.

New applications for captives are being developed all the time and are worth evaluating for your particular risk-management situation. Consulting a professional risk management advisor with captive expertise will provide insight into options for your specific needs.

Captive Insight

For examples of how captives work in specific industries, go to www.takencaptive.com and enter the phrase: "industry" in the "**Captive Insight**" box.

Chapter 2: Why form a captive?

To understand the potential benefits of forming a captive insurance company, it is helpful to first recognize that the decision to establish a captive is not a decision to abandon the commercial insurance market. Every company that operates a captive also carries various forms of commercial insurance. In a well-designed strategy, the two methods work together to provide the greatest benefits to an organization.

It's also important to recognize that the key principle behind the captive insurance concept—self-insuring some of your risks—is already practiced in some form or another by every company in existence. Said another way, no company regardless of its size or sophistication has commercial insurance coverage for 100% of its risk. This happens for a variety of reasons:

- Some companies decide to pay losses up to a certain amount and purchase insurance to cover the claims that are over that amount. This is often referred to as a *self-insured retention* and is similar to choosing a high deductible on your auto-insurance policy. You decide to choose a deductible of $1,000 to lower your premium payment from what it would be if that deductible were $500 In essence, you are agreeing to self-insure the first $1,000 of loss you may incur.

- Some companies may not know that insurance exists to cover certain potential losses and therefore, they self-insure that risk by default.
- Some may not be able to obtain insurance coverage even though it does exist. This could happen for many reasons. A risk associated with a particular segment of an industry could become too volatile for insurance companies to underwrite it. A company's loss history for a certain type of risk could be too excessive to secure adequate coverage.
- Some companies may be in an industry where historical claims were so high (e.g., completed operations coverage for developers) that it was preferable to self-insure the risk versus paying large premiums to the traditional carriers. We found this to be the case when developers were being charged $1.8 million in premiums for a $2 million policy.
- Some companies may simply be unaware of certain risks to which they are exposed and therefore they never even consider obtaining commercial coverage for those risks.
- Some insurance that a company could use may simply not exist in a form that is adequate to meet the company's needs.

When companies self-insure a portion of their risk—intentionally or otherwise—they are operating outside the confines of the commercial-insurance market because at some level, the traditional insurance market did not fit their risk-financing needs. A well-planned captive strategy will work *with* insurance markets in ways that allow organizations to achieve greater financial control and better management of their risks. This is possible because the insurer underwrites its own risks based on its own risk profile.

Captive Insight

About $0.40 - $0.50 of every premium dollar paid to commercial insurance companies goes to cover the insurers' operating expenses, overhead and profit.

Greater control

The greatest benefit a captive offers companies is significantly greater control over their risk-management program. This occurs in many ways and will be evident in the following discussion of just a few of the specific benefits of captive formation.

Improved cash flow

Beyond achieving lower premium costs, the use of captives can benefit organizations by improving cash flow. This can be achieved through developing precisely tailored coverages, improving claims handling and stabilizing insurance budgets.

Tailored coverage Earlier, we compared buying insurance to buying clothing. In our highly simplified analogy, we said buying from a commercial carrier is like buying clothes off the rack and having the choice of small, medium or large; whereas, buying through a captive is like buying clothes through a tailor who custom makes the clothes for one individual to achieve a perfect fit. A captive simply provides an organization with more risk financing options to create the best fit.

A good example of how this works is found in how small claims are handled. In the commercial insurance industry, a significant percentage of total expense is generated by what are characterized as high-frequency, low-severity claims. These are the claims that individually are de minimis, but collectively, they can account for a significant portion of an insured's total premium. A company that operates a captive can take a higher deductible to cover these small claims and purchase coverage from the captive to cover larger claims. The captive could then go to the reinsurance market to secure appropriate coverage for higher claim amounts. This saves the commercial insurer from shouldering the cost of such claims and results in a lower premium for the insured.

So why go to the trouble of setting up and funding a captive when you could just self-insure the risk? Isn't the result the same? The short answer to the second question is "No, there are definite differences between the two strategies that are worth exploring." We'll answer the first question by reviewing some of the most prominent reasons why organizations choose to establish and run captives. Within the discussion we'll also present scenarios where captive formation may not make sense.

Key benefits of establishing a captive
There are many reasons an organization chooses to form a captive. The best way to fully understand the specific opportunities and benefits for your particular organization is to consult with a risk management advisor who has expertise in the captive, traditional, and the alternative risk transfer insurance markets. Such a professional would likely gather some initial information, evaluate the organization's risk-management goals and then, if it appears a captive insurance strategy is at least a realistic possibility, recommend conducting a formal feasibility study. This process is an essential component of determining the projected return on the investment made to establish and manage a captive. After all, forming a captive is a risk-financing strategy. If the benefits are strong enough to meet or exceed the organization's internal ROI requirements, then captive formation warrants serious consideration. Although the package of benefits behind each captive will be unique to the particular organization it serves, there are certain benefits that are relatively universal.

Improved claims handling and reporting The premiums a company pays to a commercial insurer are based in large measure on industry-average claim-processing costs. The claims your company incurs are handled by the insurance company's claim administrators. This will be either the insurer's own administrators or more often, a contracted third-party administrator (or "TPA"). How well the TPA performs in terms of the time and cost to resolve claims will be a key factor in determining your premium costs. The challenge for you is that although there may be steps you could take to have a positive impact on those costs, you have no control over the TPA. Caseloads for claim managers are notoriously well in excess of anything they could effectively handle on a consistent basis. Decisions that could expedite claim resolution are routinely delayed. Claim settlement strategies that might be appropriate for your organization are ignored in favor of traditional routine. Opportunities to provide input in any meaningful way on important claim-management decisions are effectively nonexistent. In the end, you get results that are often not based on your needs, but rather, results based on the insurer's or TPA's needs. As a consequence, there is no real opportunity to impact the cost allocated to you for managing your claims.

Contrast this scenario with one that puts you in charge of setting claim-management policy, influencing claim-management strategy and ultimately having a direct impact on claim-management costs. This is the opportunity that a captive presents because it takes away the commercial-insurer layer between you and the claim manager (whether that manager is in-house or contracted).

Stabilized budgets One of the primary goals of our consulting practice is helping clients develop a strategy that allows them to take a measured approach to understanding and insuring their risks. Chief among those risks for many of our clients is financial risk; that is, risk of the unexpected interruption of cash flow, decrease in stock price or loss of earnings. Just as there are many types of financial risk, there are a variety of ways to manage them. The methods fall within three primary categories: avoid the risk, retain the risk or transfer the risk. Avoiding the risk through business-process or business-structure measures is always a preferable strategy whenever it is possible. But to the extent that it is not possible to avoid risk altogether, a company must decide whether it will retain the risk or transfer it.

If a company chooses to retain the risk, it should do so only after complete evaluation of the alternatives. A competent actuary should be retained to perform an analysis of level of risk and potential losses, as defined by potential frequency and severity of the insured-against event.

If a company chooses to transfer the risk to a traditional, commercial-insurance carrier, that company will be among many others who are insured by the same carrier. These other companies will represent a wide variety of industries and will present loss profiles that vary widely in type, frequency and severity. Despite this non-homogeneous pooling of risk, premiums may be uniformly imposed without reflecting the diversity in level of risk. This means companies with excellent safety records, great training and loss ratios far below the average in their industry will pay the same premium as companies with much higher loss histories. If, on the other hand, a company chooses to retain its risk inside a captive, the premiums will be based exclusively on that company's unique loss profile.

Incentive to control losses
While no one who is trying to run a profitable business begrudges a commercial carrier's profit motives, everyone wants to be treated fairly. This is certainly true for any company working to lower costs through careful risk-management planning and practice. If those efforts do not result in lower premium rates, then the insured believes there may be no economic reason to control losses. Conversely, when premi-

ums are established based exclusively on one organization's loss experience, and that experience is better than the average experience in the market, the company will realize lower-than-average premium costs.

A captive insurer does not have the same operating expense structure, overhead, or profit requirements of a commercial carrier. Moreover, a captive does not have to maintain higher average rates to ensure it can cover the losses associated with the high-risk members of its pool of insured. A captive's concern is sharply focused on one company as opposed to the entire industry, thereby allowing it to directly reflect that company's efforts to lower insurance costs through better risk-management. Through a captive strategy, improving risk management practices will directly impact the insured's cost of insurance.

Direct access to wholesale reinsurance markets
Reinsurance is coverage purchased by commercial insurance companies. When an insurance company assumes its insureds' risks, it often does not retain those risks for itself—at least not completely. Instead, it obtains its own insurance to compensate it for the claims it may have to pay on behalf of its insureds.

Reinsurance is purchased by insurance companies at what amounts to wholesale rates. When a company's insurance program requires reinsurance, that coverage must be secured through a commercial insurance company who buys it at wholesale and sells it to the company at retail. Because a captive is an insurance company, it can go directly to the reinsurance market and purchase coverage at the wholesale rates. The captive eliminates the commercial insurer as the middleman and allows a business direct access to global reinsurance markets. For many companies, the savings can be substantial. The direct access to reinsurers saves all of the fees paid to agents, wholesalers, and brokers, as well as the profit markup that the first-level insurer would normally earn. In addition to the fa-

vorable pricing, the company (through its captive) will also retain much more control over the choice of the most appropriate reinsurance partner.

Positive tax benefits

As pointed out in the first chapter, the deductibility of premiums is a very important benefit of establishing and running a
captive. Companies who have been self-insuring at least a portion of their risk will understand the benefits immediately.

With traditional self-insurance, companies only get a deduction for claims paid. This is very important when looking at
the overall cost of a self-insurance program, since most companies fund future liabilities using today's dollars. For example,
if a client pays $50,000 per month into the fund and uses only
$200,000 for claims, at the end of the year, it has $400,000
($50,000*12 =$600,000-$200,000=$400,000) in a trust that
cannot be deducted and would be treated as earnings. The trust
would ultimately be used to pay claims and reduce premiums
in the future. Nevertheless, after having to fund the trust in the
first place, the business then has to pay taxes on the
$400,000.00 remaining in the fund at the end of the year. This
means that a company may end up incurring more expense because it had fewer claims! It's counter-intuitive, but true. But
the bleeding doesn't stop here. There are other ancillary costs
of self-insured programs that must be considered.

Let's say a company creates a partially self-insured medical
program. It incurs two additional costs, the premium for the
excess policy, and the cost of creating and administering the
ERISA fund that is used to "warehouse" the retention funds
until they are required. These consequential expenses, coupled
with the tax limitations, can add hundreds of thousands of dollars to the cost of running a good self-insurance program.

Now let's assume we have a captive in place. The captive gets
a current deduction to fund reserves for future liabilities. When

a captive is utilized to pre-fund a business' high-frequency, low-severity claims, the business takes a current deduction for this pre-funding. In addition, the captive gets to deduct the cost of covering these claims if it has reinsured them. If the business had instead used some form of traditional self-insurance such as an equity fund to cover catastrophic losses, it would have had to reserve a significant dollar amount which would not be tax-deductible until losses occurred and were paid.

The tax impact of operating a captive is very complex and should be considered only with the advice of a competent accountant with a background in captive insurance. We address tax issues in greater detail in chapter 6.

Other benefits
There are many other benefits to including a captive insurance company in an overall risk-management strategy. Some of these include:

- Increased insurance coverage as well as capacity
- Flexibility with funding and underwriting
- Reduced deductible levels for operating units
- Better allocation capabilities
- Additional negotiating leverage for underwriters
- Creation of a market (such as pollution liability) where there is no established market;
- Additional investment income to help fund losses
- Greater stability in coverage and pricing;
- Reduction in the cost of insuring certain high-quality risks
- Reduction in expenses associated with transferring risk
- Enhanced asset protection/estate-planning/wealth transfer

Captives are not for everyone
Despite their advantages, it is important to point out that captives are not right for every organization. Unfortunately, this

doesn't keep promoters from convincing organizations to use captives in inadvisable ways.

I am continually surprised at how many organizations are led to believe they can use a captive in ways that range from being wrong for their business to being simply illegal. For example, I spend much of my time speaking to attorney-, accountant-, and insurance-professional associations. As a result of my 30-40 presentations per year, we are blessed to be seen as a resource for these groups. I recently got a call from an attorney in California whose client just signed an engagement letter to form a captive with a national promoter. The captive was an offshore captive and the policy the client's captive would write is terrorism insurance. I told their attorneys I needed more facts. Once they started describing that the client manufactured high-end, handcrafted musical instruments in a remote town of California with a population of less than 10,000, it did not make sense. With annual profit of $2,000,000, it was ridiculous to think the IRS would designate $1,200,000 in terrorism insurance premium an "ordinary necessary business expense." In this case, the IRS would not even have to challenge the legitimacy of the captive insurance company; they could simply outright deny the deduction for the insurance.

Captive Insight

A **Promoter** is an organization or individual who creates and markets alternative risk-financing strategies often using risk financing tools like captive insurance companies. While many of these promoters are legitimate, extreme caution is recommended as there are too many examples of promoters leading companies into fraudulent or otherwise illegal schemes. As always, the best strategy is to seek advice from a competent, well-experienced professional.

The very next day, we got a call from two anesthesiologists from the other coast. They went to a seminar by a national promoter and got very excited at the prospects of a captive. They had all but agreed to do it when they talked to their attorney. The attorney referred them to us and we had a brief conversation. Here is what our fact finding revealed:

- The proposed captive domicile was offshore,
- the owners were each anesthesiologists with two employees, and
- they are both looking at funding $1,200,000 in sexual harassment insurance premiums.

I told them I didn't feel the IRS would think $1,200,000 in premiums for this coverage would be justified.

With the right professional guidance, a company can relatively quickly learn the specific potential benefits to operating a captive. It can also learn the potential pitfalls. The reality is that running a captive is running an insurance company. It must be taken seriously and handled professionally. If what someone is trying to sell you doesn't look or feel like a legitimate insurance operation, get a second opinion from a professional before making any significant decisions. As with anything else, if it seems too good to be true, it probably is.

Chapter 3: What kinds of risk can be underwritten by a captive?

One of the most attractive advantages of a captive insurance company over traditional insurance is that the captive can underwrite almost any type of risk the captive owner desires. The important qualification is that it must be commercially reasonable—but it doesn't have to be commercially available. In fact, this very advantage drives many to establish a captive. A business may have a specific risk that is either unique to the market or not common enough for the market to have enough experience with the risk to be comfortable underwriting it. In this common occurrence, self-insurance is the only option a business has unless that business operates a captive.

Another advantage to having the captive write insurance is the availability of flexible terms. If you would rather pay premiums once per year, no problem; if you want to pay premiums once a month, no problem; if you want to structure a three-year policy term, no problem—flexibility rules the day.

Self insurance

When considering what policies would be appropriate for a captive to write, looking to the risks that the company currently self insures is a good place to start. With a captive, the business can identify those risks it currently self-insures and write policies to cover those risks without concern for traditional market limitations. In other words, the captive looks at the specific experience and risk profile of one company—not the entire market—to determine the appropriate coverage and premium levels. This is in contrast to the traditional market approach which looks at the broad market as opposed to the individual company to determine its coverages and term-flexibility.

You may be thinking this all sounds great, but are wondering exactly what kinds of coverage can be written and what are the limitations? First, it's important to understand that there are certainly types of coverages that are better suited for a captive. These are identified in the table below:

Coverages for Captive Consideration
• Low frequency/low severity risks • High-frequency/low severity risks • Low-frequency/high severity risks coupled with a stop-loss strategy • Risks with large established claims data and existing market of re-insurers • Risks where premiums to policy limits are very close • Risks that the company manages better than those in its industry • Currently self-insured risks

Low frequency/low severity claims

Sometimes it doesn't make sense to carry traditional insurance for claims that rarely occur and even when they do occur they are always of low-severity. Traditional insurance might not be available or it may be expensive since the carriers may charge a minimum amount for the coverage. In this case, an appropriate captive policy can balance the need for coverage and the need for appropriate premium pricing based on the individual organization's risk profile.

High-frequency/low severity claims

Some companies experience a high number of low-severity (or low-cost) claims. Purchasing insurance coverage in the traditional market for this type of claim can be expensive because of the high-frequency nature of the loss history. A captive can make appropriate adjustments thereby reducing the overall cost of financing the risk.

Low-frequency/high severity coupled with a stop-loss strategy

When claims related to a particular risk occur very infrequently but the potential loss is severe, companies often find themselves paying very high premiums for events that rarely if ever occur. For those companies who have programs or procedures in place to reduce or eliminate the risk of such claims and who wish to reduce the cost of financing whatever underlying risk actually exists, a captive is often a good alternative. This works, however, only when there is a sound stop-loss strategy in place to ensure that if a severe claim does occur, there is appropriate excess coverage to handle it.

Risks with large established claims data and existing market of re-insurers

Most captives rely on reinsurance to handle much of the risk shifting. When there is an existing strong market for the reinsurance sought and there is well-established claims data, there is a good chance that the reinsurance will be very competitively priced and easy to secure. In this case, there is a good chance the overall program to underwrite these risks using a captive will be more financially attractive to the insured than simply buying traditional insurance.

Risks where premiums to policy limits are very close

If you are purchasing coverage from a traditional carrier and the premiums you are paying are not too different than your policy limits, you would likely benefit from having the captive underwrite that risk. First, the captive coverage will be less expensive because even for the same policy, the captive's overhead is much lower than the traditional carrier. Second, you are getting almost no benefit from the traditional insurance if you are paying out about as much as you would hope to get back in the event of a loss. You are much better off paying the premium to yourself (i.e., to your captive) taking the deduction and then investing the money according to your captive's investment policy.

Risks that the company manages better than those in their industry

A large interstate trucking company has achieved a significantly better safety record than the average comparable-size company for the past five years. Each year, the company enhances its safety program which already has a full-time dedicated staff of ten people. Every quarter, the company requires its drivers to attend two-day safety courses which include classroom and practical safety training. The safety department staff reviews all Department of Transportation and National Highway Traffic Safety Administration reports, studies, bulletins and statistics to ensure any new findings or risks are incorporated into the company's safety training programming. The company enforces a no-tolerance safety policy which includes immediate termination for specified safety violations. As a result of its efforts, the company has experienced sharply fewer claims than any other trucking company in their category. However, despite these efforts, the company's insurance premium payments are only slightly lower than their competitors. The standard industry response to their consistent inquiry about why they are not seeing any significant improvement in their premium rates based on their performance is simply that the industry is seeing increased truck traffic and in many segments, increased claims. The company is told that these risks must be incorporated into the overall risk profile and that although their results have been exemplary, the underwriters need to see more than five years performance to ensure that this performance is not an anomaly. Here is an example of where the trucking company would benefit from having a captive write liability coverage. Clearly, the company's results can be linked to their professional and aggressive approach to safety. The insurance industry is in effect using this company's inflated premiums to cover the cost of claims incurred by less-diligent insureds in their category.

When your company has figured out a way to manage risk significantly better than others in your industry, writing coverage for that risk through a captive should be a consideration.

Self-insured risks
There are risks your company is currently self insuring. Some of these risks are obvious to you; for example, you may decide that for certain risks where you have a history of frequent, small claims, you'd rather pay the claims directly instead of relying on insurance coverage. However, because you want to make sure you are covered in the event one of those small claims becomes a very large claim, you keep traditional coverage but maintain a high deductible. So, effectively, you are self-insuring your claims up to a certain "retention" level. You may even have excess or catastrophic coverage that goes beyond that initial policy limit.

Figure 3.1 - Self-insured retention model

Self-insured Retention Model

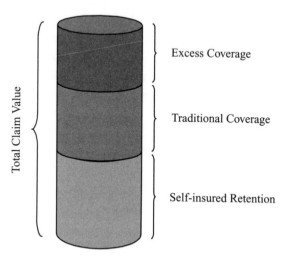

So what's the benefit to self-insuring small claims? Why is that a better alternative than simply paying a small deductible and letting the carrier cover and manage most of the claims? First, there is control. If the insurance company is not involved, you have freedom to manage and settle those claims as you see fit. You can set policy, determine who adjusts the claims, establish the settlement-authority levels, and so on. Second, those claims don't directly impact the cost of your insurance (usually). Generally speaking, your policy rates are going to be based in large part on claims against the policy. Third, you can still retain catastrophic coverage; that is, a layer of protection that can provide necessary levels of predictability for your company. But wait a minute. Doesn't this look familiar? You are managing your small claim activity, setting policy, paying out claims and purchasing "excess" or "catastrophic" coverage (i.e., high-deductible coverage). That looks a whole lot like you are running a captive insurance company. The only thing missing is the premium payments to deduct as a business expense. Essentially, you're already doing the work that a captive insurance operator would be doing, but you're just not getting the tax benefit.

Let me give you a practical example of this potential benefit. We have a client that had a partially self-insured medical insurance program for their business. Before they went self-insured, their premiums for a PPO plan were $60,000 per month. They have very young, single employees so they decided to go with a partially self-funded plan. They retain the first $25,000 of all claims per employee and purchase Transamerica insurance to cover the excess of loss. They pay $15,000 per month for the Transamerica excess policy and they are required to put $32,000 per month in an ERISA sinking fund. After claims paid, last year they had an additional $300,000 in the trust. Since this was not deductible, they had to pay corporate taxes on this additional money left in the company. A captive could eliminate the extra tax burden on the company using the captive to insure the first $25,000 per employee. The captive can also negotiate the specific stop-loss (excess coverage for each employee) and the annual aggregate stop-loss (captive total payout) from the reinsurance market. Without a captive insurance company you are only able to buy what is in essence a high deductible plan, not a reinsurance contract. The high deductible policy has most of the retail charges and commissions heaped in so the savings are minimal.

We can see then how a captive can be used to replace existing risks that are self-insured up to a certain claim level. But what other coverages are appropriate for a captive insurance company?

Alternative coverage options

The insurance your company is currently purchasing through the traditional market likely includes coverages such as general liability, property, workers' compensation, product liability, directors' and officers' and auto. Many captive owners are perfectly comfortable with these coverages and wouldn't consider moving them to a captive. However, there are times when the terms, conditions, or coverage levels that are available in the market do not meet a company's needs.

This can happen for a variety of reasons. For example, there are times when a particular industry is hit with abnormally high losses which trigger market increases in premium rates. When that happens, all organizations in the industry are impacted regardless of their specific loss experience. Some companies decide that it would be more economical to have the captive underwrite this risk because the premium levels would accurately reflect the organization's actual loss experience and risk and not that of the entire industry.

If you are looking for options for a potential captive to write, as it turns out, there are many. Once again, provided the coverage is commercially reasonable, it can be written by a captive. For example, captives will often write some form of liability coverage. Some of the most popular liability insurance carried by captives include: workers compensation insurance, general liability insurance, professional liability insurance and directors and officers liability insurance.

Other liability coverages include errors and omissions, professional liability, performance liability and product liability insurance. Captives will also frequently write coverages such as employment practices liability insurance, patent- and trademark-infringement liability insurance and environmental liability insurance.

Because an organization's individual liability coverage needs are often unique, it's important to carefully tailor the program. This means structuring the policy to cover the unique liability needs for the insured and then retain excess coverages appropriate to each coverage need. A five-person dental practice with a highly stable employee base may be comfortable with its captive retaining a high-level of the risk of employment practices liability. However, a 10,000 employee retail chain with high employee turnover may decide to have the captive cover the initial risk only up to a modest dollar amount and retain excess coverage for the rest.

An organization may also write highly customized policies that don't exist in the traditional market. For example, a traditional general liability policy may be ill-suited to cover sexual misconduct losses incurred by a company that operates a chain of daycare centers. If this is a risk for the organization, a policy can be custom tailored by the captive to address it.

Likewise, a traditional business interruption policy may not adequately protect an organization for a delay in product launch. For a software developer with frequent new product offerings, a launch delay can have serious financial consequences. The company's captive can write insurance coverage to compensate for losses associated with such delays. Business interruption can happen for a myriad of reasons as unique and complex as the organizations experiencing them. A parts manufacturer for the automobile industry could be preferred because of specialized equipment. If that equipment breaks, there may be no quick or easy fix thereby resulting in loss. A captive can write a policy that will cover losses caused by the out-of-service equipment and can even cover losses to the business resulting from losing a major customer because of the equipment breakdown.

The risk of loss of trade secrets and other confidential information is greater than it has ever been. Traditional policies may well come up short in providing an organization with the protection it needs, or the coverage offered may simply be much broader than the company requires. Either way, a carefully tailored policy written by a captive can address precisely the needs of a particular organization. Let's say a large consulting firm frequently handles its clients' highly confidential business documents—strategies, financial plans, competitive secrets, etc. Because of the practical advantages of current wireless communications technology, the consulting company chooses to move a lot of confidential information through wireless transmission. It wants coverage to protect it from loss caused by the interception of such transmission. Let's say the standard policy to cover this kind of loss in the traditional market also covers a variety of other forms of loss that are not relevant to this consulting firm—or the wireless interception coverage is not extensive enough. The captive can not only write just the coverage that the firm needs, it can also make sure that coverage addresses exactly the potential losses anticipated.

Captives are increasingly finding practical application in the employee-benefit market as well. Some companies are now offering voluntary employee benefit programs through their captive insurance companies. These include supplemental health and life coverages. Why not just go direct to the traditional market for these coverages? The captive can provide benefits at a lower cost than is available in the retail market and because it has a very low overhead, it can pass the savings onto the company's employees. Captives can also write post-retirement medical, dental, disability and life insurance policies—again saving the company and the company's retirees money.

Practically speaking, the options are limitless. Understanding your company's risks and defining the most appropriate coverage scenario that would address those risks in the most cost-effective way is what captives do best. Understanding those risks and then drafting and administering relevant policies covering those risks is part of effective captive management.

Chapter 4: Structuring a captive

When you are satisfied that the benefits of operating a captive are worth a deeper analysis, one key question will be, "What type of captive is best for my organization?" As you begin evaluating alternatives, you will quickly discover substantial differences in the various captive types and structures of captives. You'll also notice that these differences have a substantial impact on the captive owner's financials. For that reason, your CFO, attorney and tax advisor will be critical members of the team that evaluates the efficacy of captive formation. In particular, a key area of focus will be the tax implications of operating a captive. While tax considerations alone should never drive a captive-formation decision, they can't be ignored and almost always play an important role in structure decisions.

Main organizational types

In most cases, when a captive insurance company is formed in a U.S. domicile, it is organized as a stock, mutual, limited liability, or reciprocal company. Captives formed offshore are most often stock or mutual companies.

A **stock insurer** is an incorporated organization that issues and sells stock to raise capital. Like many corporations, profits generated by a stock company are typically distributed to shareholders through dividends. They can also be returned to insureds through return of premium or renewal credits. As a corporation, a stock company benefits from limited liability.

A **mutual insurer**, unlike a stock company, does not issue stock. It is owned by policyholders, called "members," who contribute surplus to fund the captive. When there is a profit, that profit is returned to the policyholders in the form of return of premium. Like a stock insurer, a mutual company is an incorporated entity which means members enjoy limited liability.

A **limited liability company (LLC)** sits somewhere between a stock company and a mutual. An LLC does not issue stock but it does offer limited liability to its members. In the world of captives, it is a relatively new structure that is gaining increased acceptance. For example, it was approved by Vermont as an eligible legal entity in the 2004 legislative session.

A **reciprocal** organization is an unincorporated association that is licensed by the domicile in which it is organized as a captive insurance company. A reciprocal's subscribers contribute surplus, agree to share risks with one another and are governed by a Subscribers' Advisory Committee (SAC). The reciprocal's operating authority is granted to an attorney in fact by each of the subscribers. Any profits or income from investments can be allocated by the SAC to the reciprocal's Subscriber Savings Account (SSA). One of the main advantages of operating a reciprocal under U.S. tax law is the annual deductibility of profits allocated to the SSA. Profits later distributed out of the SSA to subscribers pass tax free.

Main structure types
In addition to the organizational form the company must de-

cide on what type of captive to form. Ultimately, a feasibility study will identify the various forms of capture structures the company should consider when forming a captive. This is just one of the many functions of a feasibility study which is discussed in greater detail in Chapter 8.

The following discussion outlines the features of the most frequently used structures.

Single-parent captive

A single-parent captive is a separate legal entity formed as a subsidiary of another legal entity referred to as the "parent" (see figure 3.1). The captive is formed to insure the risks of its parent and parent-affiliated companies. If appropriately licensed and capitalized, a single-parent captive may also insure the risks of third parties.

The capital required to form and operate a single-parent captive is provided by the parent. The parent will maintain complete control over underwriting terms, policy language, reinsurance decisions and investment policy.

Single-parent captives are often referred to as "pure" captives, but the two concepts are not synonymous. A pure captive is typically defined by domiciles as either a single-parent captive or a group-owned captive that underwrites the risks of the owner(s) only (with limited exceptions). Some characterize pure captives as captives that do not have a commercial purpose. That is, they do not operate to make profit selling insurance to insureds unrelated to the owner(s).

Figure 4.1 – Single-parent captive structure

Single-parent Captive

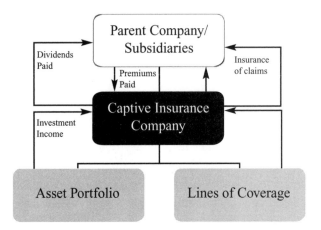

To be effective, a single-parent captive requires a long-term commitment from its owner(s). Legislation varies from jurisdiction to jurisdiction, but most require capital and surplus of at least $100,000.

Typical single parent captive formation example:
Real estate developer

A classic fit for single parent captives are real estate developers. Developer A would create an entity to act as its insurance company. All of the single purpose LLCs that hold ownership interest in developments would purchase insurance from the developer's captive insurance company. If structured properly, this would allow the developer to take deductions to pre-fund losses that may occur in the future. If those losses do not materialize, the captive would have underwriting profit on that block of business.

Risk retention group captive

A risk retention group (RRG) is a captive insurance company owned by multiple businesses with similar insurance needs.

They were first allowed with the passing of the federal Liability and Risk Retention Act (LRRA) which allowed groups to form an insurance company and to be chartered in one state but engage in the business of providing insurance in all states in which they become registered and licensed.

Although the RRG is required to comply with the laws of the domicile in which it is organized, federal regulation eases some of the financial reporting and filing fees associated with becoming an admitted carrier in the various states in which it provides coverage. This gives a risk retention group the ability to provide more cost effective insurance for its members/owners. A typical RRG issues polices to its members and retains some risk. The RRG would determine how much risk they wanted to assume and would purchase reinsurance to cover losses in excess of their risk appetite. Most of the RRGs require their members not only to pay premium to the captive, but require them to make a capital contribution to the insurance company as well.

Typical risk retention group captive formation example: Medical groups

Doctors face high premiums for medical malpractice insurance. Many medical groups have banded together and formed insurance companies to bring down the high cost of this insurance. In a typical scenario, doctors (let's use 20 as an example) all form an insurance company to provide $1,000,000-$5,000,000 coverage. The doctors would have a deductible of $25,000 and the captive would insure the doctors from $25,000 to some aggregate limit like $250,000. On any specific claim the captive would be responsible for $225,000. The RRG would purchase reinsurance to cover the liability above $250,000. In theory, the premiums should be lower—the doctors may have better control over the claims and payments. The RRG should also achieve efficiency by creating underwriting guidelines to include good-risk and exclude bad-risk doctors.

Rental captive

A rental captive is formed by investors to provide captive services to organizations that want the advantages of a captive but do not or cannot form their own captive. The rental captive typically "rents" its capital and surplus to the policyholder organization for a fee and provides its own administration and reinsurance services.

In this model, the policyholder business is insured by the captive but usually has much less control over the insurer's operations than is the case in other more traditional structures. In addition to charging a fee, a rental captive usually requires some form of collateral to protect it from any underwriting losses attributable to the renter.

This structure—which is often formed as a segregated cell captive—can be appealing to smaller organizations that cannot afford the start-up costs of forming a captive. Nevertheless, the insured's lack of control and some unsettled questions regarding tax treatment can be significant disadvantages.

Segregated cell/protected cell captives

Some captive insurance companies are structured to allow a legal segregation of underwriting accounts (or "cells") from each other (see figure 3.2). Segregated cell companies can be single-parent captives, rental captives or group captives. The formal requirements for structuring a segregated cell captive will be defined by the domicile in which the captive is licensed to operate.

Capital requirements and bankruptcy protection are two reasons captive owners choose this structure.

For example, a company operating a segregated-cell captive will be required to capitalize each cell separately based on actuarial calculations and the risk profile of that cell. When the sum of the capital requirements for all cells is less than the capital requirement would be if the captive were structured without cells, the segregated cell structure becomes an attractive alternative.

Figure 4.2 – Segregated-cell captive structure

Segregated-cell Captive

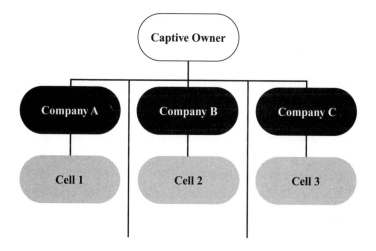

The segregated-cell structure may provide some financial protection in that it can allow the assets in a cell to remain protected (sometimes called "bankruptcy remote") from creditors of the captive in the event of a bankruptcy.

A note of caution however when it comes to segregated cell captives: There are currently a few large insurance companies offering a segregated cell concept. In order to create the segregated cell, the carriers require the cell owner to fully collateralize the risk they are taking. We have seen situations where the cell captive owner needs to post letters of credit that increase each year. For example: a developer that writes a $2 million policy limit and pays $1 million in premium for that policy will be required to post the additional $1 million in a letter of credit with the carrier. Hence, the developer is giving the carrier $2 million in assets for the $2 million liability. In the second year, the developer will be faced with the same problem and will have to post additional letters of credit to the carrier. The cell captive owner can soon get into a situation where it has stacking letters of credit with no real way to exit the arrangement.

There is also a debate within the captive community on the right way to structure cell captive programs. Some take the position the IRS has not been clear on the proper way to structure the distribution and risk shifting component of the cell captive. With that in mind, we are aware of the guidance the IRS is working on in an attempt to clarify its position. Cell captive structures are relatively new and the protection pitched by many promoters has yet to be tested in court.

Association captive insurers
These organizations underwrite the risks of members of an industry or trade association. Liability risks such as medical malpractice are frequently insured using this structure.

Agency captive insurers
Formed by insurance brokers, agency captives allow the brokers-owners to invest in low-risk portions of their insurance book of business. These captive insurers exercise a great deal of control over the level of risk they will insure.

Special purpose vehicles (SPV)
SPVs are captive reinsurers used by other insurers to securitize risk. They issue reinsurance contracts to their parent insurers and then sell the risk on the capital markets by way of a bond issue.

Structuring examples for different industries
Captives are clearly not just for the largest companies anymore. The following examples illustrate how many small to mid-size

organizations in a variety of industries are discovering the benefits of alternative risk financing.

Real estate developers

Real estate developers are faced with a very high cost of insurance. Although prices have fallen in recent years, developers are still commonly required to pay $750,000-$1,000,000 for a $1M/$2M/$2M policy (a policy that covers $1,000,000 per claim, $2,000,000 aggregate and $2,000,000 products and completed operations). For the developer, this is not a favorable way to finance risk. First, the determination of the premium cost is largely unaffected by the developer's efforts to improve its risk profile. Second, the timing of the premium payment is built to favor the insurance company.

Efforts to improve risk profile Many developers work hard at building a quality product and improving jobsite safety which results in fewer claims. Unfortunately, that record of success isn't fully reflected in the premium costs. Remember that insurance companies count on being able to shift and distribute their risk over many insureds. That means some in the risk pool are effectively paying more for coverage than they should while others are paying less. Those developers operating in the traditional market who hope that improved loss rates will result in significantly lower premium expense are often disappointed. This creates the opportunity (or necessity) for considering alternatives to the traditional risk financing strategies.

Impact of timing In most cases, when a developer makes a $1,000,000 premium payment for a $1M/$2M/$2M policy, the liability portion may only cost a few hundred thousand dollars of this premium. The majority of the premium is to cover completed operations (construction defects). Here is where the timing favors the insurance company. Despite the fact that the developer is required to pay premiums on day one, a completed operations claim can't be made until after construction is complete—a process that typically takes 24 to 36 months. Claims on completed operations can be made for another 10 to 15 years depending on the state laws where the construction took place. With the average litigated claim taking 2 to 3 years to resolve, the insurance company can have upwards of 15 to 20 years to grow the developer's $1,000,000 premium to the policy limits (see figure 3.3).

Captive Insight

For more examples of captive structures for different industries go to www.takencaptive.com and enter the phrase: "examples" in the "**Captive Insight**" box.

It's easy to see how the developer is better off being the insurer. First, the developer's premium cost will be based on its own loss history. Second, it can keep the premium dollars invested in its own account until required to pay claims. Third, having direct access to the reinsurance market means a lower total cost of insurance.

For our developer clients, we often structure a captive to take advantage of the falling cost of reinsurance. Here's how it works: The captive writes a policy to cover the first $250,000 loss per claim up to a maximum loss of $1,000,000. To cover its risk, the captive then purchases reinsurance at a cost of about $200,000. For the captive, pricing the premium is more about evaluating the actual risk of one insured. The insurance company, however, prices the policy so that the premium grows to whatever the limit is by the time a claim must be paid.

Figure 4.3 - Traditional insurance: real estate development

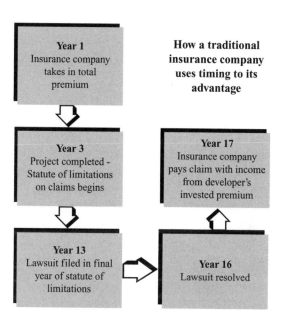

Executive leasing firms

Companies who lease executive talent typically carry significant health insurance costs. As an example, one of our clients was paying $1,300,000 for health insurance. The business owner did not know what the utilization of the health plan was, but felt it was low. The health carrier was reluctant to release the claims payment history to the client, but in the end, had to release the data. For years, the average annual total amount this company used under its policy was about $100,000. By using a captive insurer, we helped this company dramatically reduce its insurance costs.

Our strategy was to implement a partially self-insured medical plan. The firm self insured the first $30,000 of loss per employee per year up to a $1,000,000 maximum for all claims. The company had to purchase two types of insurance policies.

The first provided coverage above $30,000 per participant. This coverage limited the liability on any one employee or catastrophic event. The second type of insurance was a stop loss policy. This limited the total payments of the company to $1,000,000 per year. Once the employer paid out up to the stop loss limit, they were through.

The monthly cost for the aggregate coverage and the stop loss coverage was $15 per employee and $38 per family. The captive was reinsured by an A-rated carrier. This structure will bring in the expected claims and insurance cost for the medical coverage to under $300,000 per year. That means if the company's loss history is consistent with the past several years, it will save about $1,000,000 per year. Even if the company experiences extraordinary losses and it hits all maximum claim limits, its total insurance cost would not exceed $1,3000,000—exactly what it was paying under the traditional insurance model! That is, if this company experienced catastrophic losses—unlike anything even close to its historical losses—it would be no worse off financially than if it continued under its previous risk-financing strategy.

There are other benefits to this alternative risk-financing strategy. We have structured the captive so that it is owned by the company's executives (along with the owners of the company). This creates an additional incentive for the executives to adopt initiatives that create and reinforce a healthier workforce. The executives keep a close eye on the performance of the captive because over time, they hope it is profitable. When they leave the company, they sell their shares of the captive and the proceeds are taxed at the long-term capital gains rates. Alternatively, if they were paid a traditional cash bonus, that would be taxed as ordinary income.

Medical
One of our clients is an anesthesiologist practice with fifteen anesthesiologists. When we started working with them, they

were paying $800,000 per year for medical malpractice coverage. Fourteen of the fifteen physicians in the practice represented a very good risk—there were no claims. The one exception had all the practice's claims—three in two years.

We structured a captive and had the captive purchase reinsurance at a cost of $185,000 dollars per year. The reinsurance excluded the physician who had incurred the claims. We had the captive write insurance for $1,600,000 in premium to cover all the physicians for claims up to $1,000,000 per claim and $5,000,000 in the annual aggregate.

All the physicians paid extra into the captive. If the captive has an underwriting profit, each physician will be able to take out more than $1,000,000 each in ten years.

In this case, we were able to use the alternative-risk financing strategy to isolate one high-risk physician from the group while still covering the practice's risks and creating a wealth-management instrument.

These are just a few of the ways captives can be structured to creatively and effectively manage organizations' risk-financing needs. With the help of a risk management advisor with expertise in alternative risk-financing strategies, you can evaluate whether a captive makes sense for your organization, and if so, which structure is most appropriate.

Chapter 5: Which domicile is best?

Selecting the domicile for your captive is a very important decision that should never be made in a vacuum. Many factors that can have a significant impact on whether your captive will (or even can) meet your risk-financing needs, must be considered. A detailed analysis of the many nuances of the wide variety of domiciles is beyond the scope of this book; however, this chapter will raise some of the most important issues anyone making a domicile choice should consider with competent professional guidance. Generally, domicile considerations align under four categories:

- Legislative/regulatory considerations

- Financial considerations

- Infrastructure considerations

- Perception considerations

Captive Insight

There are more than 50 captive-friendly domiciles throughout the world. In the United States alone, there are at least 24 domiciles that recognize captive organizations. For a complete list, log on to www.TakenCaptive.com and enter the word: "domiciles" in the "Captive Insight" box.

Before we look into each set of considerations, it's worth taking a moment to discuss what it means to be "captive friendly" and why some domiciles are and some are not. When a domicile recognizes captive insurers—meaning the domicile is willing to license a captive insurance structure as an insurance organization—it is considered captive friendly. That doesn't mean, however, that it will meet your specific needs. Domiciles have been in the business of licensing captives for different amounts of time. The domiciles that have been in the captive business for a long time have naturally seen more than those who are relatively new to captive legislation. With increased experience, you can usually find an increased understanding of the captive owner's goals. Each domicile's legislators have determined what they believe to be appropriate uses of a captive. Not surprisingly, they do not all agree with one another as to the definition of "appropriate."

Vermont, for example has been very aggressive in marketing itself as the most established and most experienced captive domicile in the United States. Regarding the captive insurance industry, Vermont says:

> "Our laws and regulations keep pace with industry needs. Our legislature listens and is responsive."[i]

The state goes so far as to stake its claim as the "undisputed onshore leader" in captive insurance.[ii] But that claim is well supported. With captive regulation on the books for more than 25 years and about half of the Fortune 500 companies that operate captives doing so in Vermont, the state dominates the U.S. market.

Today, Vermont has issued about 800 captive licenses. It has taken its place as the number one U.S. domicile and the number three domicile worldwide. Hawaii comes in as the second-largest U.S. domicile with more than 200 captive licenses issued. Other popular U.S. domiciles include Arizona, Nevada and New York. As the interest in captive formation increases among companies considering alternative risk financing options, so does the number of domiciles to consider.

So, why would a state want to be a captive domicile of choice? Well, no surprise, it comes down to revenue. When companies decide to establish a captive insurance company, there are costs associated with establishing and managing the captive—some of which benefit the domicile. Domiciles also receive tax revenue. For example, Vermont receives about 2% of its general revenue from taxes paid by its captive owners on the $7 billion in premiums that pass through the state.[iii]

There are also significant investments made in the state which represent positive business development. Well over 1,000 jobs are either directly or indirectly attributed to the captive industry in Vermont; banks in the domicile benefit (about $1 billion attributed to captives is on deposit at Vermont banks), captive consultants and captive managers in the domicile benefit, attorneys in the domicile benefit, accountants and actuaries in the domicile benefit and investment advisors benefit. You get the picture—it's economic development and the potential is driving some stiff competition among domiciles.

Legislative/regulatory considerations
Although the legislation in the leading domiciles may be similar in many ways, there are some differences that may be very significant to any one particular organization so it's very im-

portant that you are getting good advice from an advisor who
has no special interest in any one particular domicile.

Regulators exercise significant freedom in determining what
lines of business can and cannot be covered by captives operating in their domicile. For example, a company that wants to
use a captive to write workers' compensation or employer liability insurance might have a difficult time in Arizona:

> "A pure captive insurer shall not provide direct coverage of
> workers' compensation or employers' liability insurance in
> another state unless the coverage is provided under a self-
> insurance program that is qualified as a self-insurance pro-
> gram under the applicable state or federal law, as
> determined by the agency or other entity that has jurisdic-
> tion over the self-insurance program."[iv]

Understanding legislative requirements of various domiciles
becomes particularly important as companies develop new
risk-transfer products or consider using captives to write non-
traditional property-casualty lines. In addition to "permitted
business," jurisdictions may differ on other key legislative or
regulatory matters such as investment restrictions, reinsurance
provisions and financial reporting requirements.

So far, our discussion has not specifically addressed onshore
versus offshore domiciles. Certainly there are many captives
located outside the U.S. (in "offshore domiciles"). The popu-
larity of the offshore domicile—at least for U.S.-owned captives—was largely driven by differences in how income,
premiums and dividends were treated from a tax perspective
when compared to a domestic captive. The other reason there
are so many offshore-domiciled captives, is that non-U.S.
domiciles have simply been around longer.

To compete with the offshore domiciles, U.S. domiciles have
worked hard to offer similar advantages. Take South Carolina

for example. On their captive insurance website is the following presentation which specifically addresses offshore captives:

"South Carolina's new captive insurance law ... offers companies ...
    all the advantages typically associated with an off-shore captive:
    • single parent, association and group captives are permitted;
    • reasonable capitalization requirements that may be met with a letter of credit;
    • coverage that includes nearly all life, accident and health lines, commercial lines and property and casualty insurance products;
    • no regulatory approval of rates and forms required;
    • no minimum premium requirement;
    • competitive corporate and premium tax structure;
    • no investment restrictions for pure captives and non-RRG industrial insured groups"[v]

As a result of its marketing efforts, South Carolina has attracted more than 175 captives since 2000.

While there may still be advantages for a particular captive to form offshore, the distinction between the two options is smaller than it has ever been. For example, not so long ago, a company that wanted tax-free premium income would have to look offshore. Today, that is available domestically (Arizona does not charge a premium tax). In addition to a few tax-treatment differences, the main reasons companies consider an offshore domicile include administrative flexibility, unique asset-protection options, access to foreign investment and proximity to reinsurers (who often headquarter in offshore domiciles). We have found that a bona fide reason to go offshore is the ability to write insurance that is not available domestically. For example, it is against public policy in the United

States to write a punitive damage policy. However, these polices are available offshore. Also, warranty policies in many
states are not considered insurance. For that reason many developers, contractors and car dealers formed captives in offshore jurisdictions.

So which is better, onshore or offshore? Well, that depends. As
you meet with your experts and advisors to evaluate the feasibility of a captive insurance company, you will begin to see
and better understand the advantages and limitations that various domiciles present for your particular needs. For the most
part, a U.S.-based company will find everything it needs domestically, but it certainly makes sense as part of the due-diligence process to evaluate the offshore options.

Financial considerations
One of the biggest initial considerations for companies evaluating different domiciles for their captive insurance company
is how much capital and surplus will be required. When a company sets up a captive, it is required to "fund" it. Every insurance authority wants assurance that captives formed in their
domicile will be able to meet the financial requirements of the
risks they are underwriting. They therefore require evidence
that the captive can pay claims made against the policies that
are written.

In addition to the capital requirement, domiciles have surplus
minimums. Surplus is an amount that is additional to what the
captive needs to meet its financial responsibilities for policies
it has underwritten. It represents additional capacity for the
captive to write new policies.

Each domicile has specific guidelines for minimum capital and
surplus. Based on those guidelines, one domicile may emerge
as a better fit for a company's particular risk profile. A careful
reading of each domicile's captive law is important. Consider
the following.

Vermont's captive law reads in part:

"No captive insurance company shall be issued a license unless it shall possess and thereafter maintain unimpaired paid-in capital and surplus of:

    (1) in the case of a pure captive insurance company, not less than $250,000.00;

    (2) in the case of an association captive insurance company, not less than $750,000.00;

    (3) in the case of an industrial insured captive insurance company, not less than $500,000.00;

    (4) in the case of a risk retention group, not less than $1,000,000.00; and

    (5) in the case of a sponsored captive insurance company, not less than $500,000.00.

(b) The commissioner may prescribe additional capital and surplus based upon the type, volume, and nature of insurance business transacted.

c) Capital and surplus may be in the form of cash or an irrevocable letter of credit issued by a bank chartered by the state of Vermont or a member bank of the Federal Reserve System and approved by the commissioner."[vi]

Arizona requires pure captive insurers to provide a minimum $250,000.00 for capital and surplus.[vii]

South Carolina sets specific limits for capital ($100,000.00) and for surplus ($150,000.00) with the total requirement of $250,000.00 matching Vermont, Arizona and Utah.

South Dakota requires $100,000.00 capital and $100,000.00 surplus.[viii]

The fact that these domiciles are very similar in their requirements is due in large part to the National Association of Insurance Commissioners, or NAIC. The NAIC can challenge any legislation that it deems to be unsound; this results in certain minimum requirements that each domicile is forced to maintain. Offshore domiciles, however, can establish very different standards as they are unaffected by the NAIC.

When you review the various U.S domicile captive legislation, you'll notice that domiciles often permit the use of letters of credit. This is true of most onshore domiciles and is particularly attractive to those companies that have available assets to support a captive but can't comfortably afford to initially commit today all the cash that may be required to pay claims later. By using non-cash assets as collateral for a letter of credit, the captive can meet the domicile's minimum capital and surplus requirements while keeping its cash available for its core business. Some regulators may even prefer a funding arrangement using a letter of credit because it could offer some greater protection over cash-funding in the event of bankruptcy. Cash sitting in an account is harder to protect from other creditors than a letter of credit held by an insurance department. You can see what Vermont requires by looking at the example irrevocable letter of credit posted on its website. It is included here as Appendix A.

Taxation - Certainly the tax impact of forming and operating a captive insurance company is a key financial concern and will be a prominent point of financial analysis. We review a variety of tax issues facing captives in chapter 5.

Infrastructure

When you are evaluating domiciles for your new captive insurance company, infrastructure is one of the most important immediate and long-term considerations. It is important to recognize that simply enacting legislation that recognizes a captive insurance structure does not make a domicile appropriate for each captive's needs. The domicile must have adequate infrastructure in place to support that legislation, and the support must be adequate for your particular needs. This is increasingly important to understand as more and more domiciles enter the captive insurance business and some may not be fully prepared.

The success of any captive is going to be based in large part on the system supporting it. That support system has basic components such as financial, legal, actuarial, operational and administrative and it starts in the domicile because there are certain administrative matters that must be handled within that jurisdiction. While some functions can be handled outside the domicile, the captive owner must be cautious. Each domicile's regulatory environment is different—sometimes in very subtle ways. Those differences are most likely going to be better understood by those service providers who are operating within that jurisdiction every day. Moreover, it's always good to know you have an advocate within the domicile that can quickly get a meeting with the regulators when issues arise.

In most cases, the jurisdictions are efficient and very helpful to the owners of newly formed captives. But an often overlooked stumbling block lies with the outside auditors many of the jurisdictions use to help scrutinize the captives within their domicile. These jurisdictions rely on these outside auditors to approve or deny the captive application without providing much guidance. As it turns out, when it comes to determining acceptable levels of risk, auditors do not always agree. It is possible for one auditor with a low-risk tolerance to require capital to support a 90% loss while another determines it is acceptable to set the capital requirement at a 75% loss. When the jurisdiction does not provide clear guidance as to its requirements, independent auditors will fill in the blanks—often with significantly different interpretations. This can create administrative bottlenecks for the captive owner if differing interpretations require revised business plans and re-calculated actuarial reports. This will add to the cost and time to form the captive.

The point is that in most cases, the captive owner will have little to no experience in forming or running an insurance company. And since the captive must be operated with the same diligence and professionalism of any insurance company, the owner must ensure it has the right service providers in place. Once you fully understand what is required, you begin to understand the importance that infrastructure plays in the choice-of-domicile decision.

Because consultants and service providers within each domicile naturally have a vested interest in pointing out the positives while overlooking or downplaying the negatives, you would be well-served to use an independent third party advisor to assist in the infrastructure-evaluation process. A qualified expert will often already have a working knowledge of the capabilities of multiple domiciles and will be able to provide an objective look at the domiciles' infrastructures as they apply to your particular needs.

Perception

There's no denying that all things being equal (and even when all things are *not* equal), some are influenced by the location of certain domiciles. After all, when it's time to schedule the next captive board meeting, would you rather be preparing for a trip to Bermuda or South Dakota? Nothing against South Dakota, but you can just imagine that you might find it a bit easier to find room on your calendar for the trip to Bermuda. You'd certainly be justified in saying that Bermuda is probably the world's premier captive domicile. After all, about 1,000 captives operate there; many of these captives represent the biggest and most sophisticated companies and there is a well-established infrastructure. But when choosing a domicile, don't overlook the impact of perception. Will you be able to defend the decision to operate an offshore subsidiary to your board of directors? If all your business is in the U.S., what will shareholders think about establishing a foreign subsidiary? Are you ready to answer the shareholder questions at the next annual meeting about the necessity of trips to exotic countries that have the (albeit unfair) reputation of being questionable tax havens?

Likewise, if your state offers strong captive legislation and it will meet your infrastructure needs, what are the legitimate business reasons to form a captive in another domicile—say Hawaii or Arizona? I'm certainly not saying that you should avoid considering a domicile because it happens to have great beaches or great golf. If it is right for your captive-insurance needs, it should be considered. Just understand that perception will come into play at some point and it is better to explore it and understand its potential impact before it becomes an issue.

Questions to ask

As you conduct your analysis of various domiciles, there are a number of matters to consider. The following is a simple list that can serve as a place to begin your inquiry.

1. *What are the domicile's legislative and regulatory philosophy, commitment and appreciation of captive insurance companies?*

   Sometimes domiciles will enact captive legislation without fully appreciating (or understanding) the captive insurance model. In fact, it can take years for a domicile to fully commit to captives. This commitment can be seen in the speed at which regulatory questions are answered through revised or amended legislation. It can also be seen in the type of legislation that is enacted—how much flexibility is provided to captive operators, how broadly or narrowly the captive legislation is interpreted, etc. If the analysis of domiciles focuses too much on single issues such as minimum capitalization and surplus requirements, other important matters that can have a big impact down the road might be missed.

2. *What lines of insurance does the domicile permit captives to write?*

   Not all domiciles permit captives to write the same coverages. Regulators accustomed to regulating only the traditional insurance industry may not be quick to draft regulation that allows companies to write very different lines of coverage. As companies realize that captive insurers can be formed to underwrite a seemingly infinite list of risks, this becomes a critical question.

3. How accessible are the captive regulators and relevant government officials?
In a market that changes as quickly as the captive insurance industry, the regulators who call the shots become very important—that means access to them becomes very important. The domiciles that have had the most success attracting captives through the years understand this point well and make it very clear that accessibility is a key priority and an,advantage for operating within their jurisdiction. However, this doesn't mean you should ignore domiciles that are relatively new to captive regulation. While Vermont and Bermuda are highly effective at linking regulators with captive owners, the same can be said by some relative newcomers such as Arizona, and Nevada.

4. What are the regulatory reporting and examination requirements?
Understand each domicile's reporting and examination requirements so that there are no surprises down the road. It's also important to know where records must be maintained. This becomes relevant to those companies that decide they want to maintain captive administrative offices in a location outside the domicile. An important point regarding administrative requirements is that less is not always best. It may appear on first blush that a domicile with less regulatory reporting and oversight requirements is preferable, and sometimes that is true. However, a domicile with surprisingly few reporting requirements might signal a lack of attention to or understanding of the intricacies of the captive-industry. It could also signal a lack of qualified staff dedicated to captive-regulation oversight. In either case, such a domicile should be approached with caution.

Many business owners welcome less government regulation in the course of their business. When looking at forming a captive, regulation is your friend. In some heavily regulated jurisdictions it is not uncommon for three actuaries to review the captive. They will review the captive owner's actuarial report, the jurisdiction's report and the outside auditor's analysis of the viability of the captive. It is this redundancy that often gives comfort to the captive owner that no detail has been missed.

People to see

Your review of domiciles should include a careful evaluation of the people who will be the closest to your captive (probably closer than you as the owner). Most captives employ a captive management company that becomes responsible for day-to-day operations such as writing policies, underwriting risks and paying claims. In addition, captives require competent legal counsel, third-party administrators and financial professionals such as auditors, actuaries and investment managers who are expert in understanding the special needs of captive insurance companies. Captive owners also need to develop strong banking relationships with institutions that understand the domicile's regulatory requirements as well as the needs of the captive.

These relationships should be carefully evaluated before a domicile decision is made—although surprisingly, this is often not the case. The evaluation process can be completed relatively quickly and is too important to overlook. A competent risk management advisor can provide some additional guidance based on experience and can make key introductions to accelerate and enhance the evaluation process.

Some issues will clearly take priority over others, but understanding what makes one domicile different than others is an important part of the feasibility and due-diligence process.

In the next chapter, we review one of the most important considerations for any captive owner—the tax implications of forming and operating a captive insurance company.

Chapter 6: What are the tax considerations?

There is little question that the tax implications of owning and operating a captive insurance company will be significant. For most organizations, the decision to insure through a captive versus a combination of traditional insurance and self insurance is significantly influenced by tax implications. Many organizations first discover this difference in tax impact from a captive promoter—especially when the tax impact is significant in a way that is beneficial to the potential captive owner. However, if your only motive in forming a captive is to gain some tax advantage, you would be well advised to reconsider.

As I point out throughout this book, there are many legitimate reasons for operating a captive. In order to do so effectively and without raising the scrutiny of the IRS and insurance regulators, you must operate your captive like an insurance company. Your captive must be appropriately capitalized; it must underwrite and actually transfer and distribute risk; it must pay claims if they are incurred, and so on. If, however, your operation is little more than a shell organization designed to provide predictable tax deductions, you should plan on an expensive and uncomfortable series of interactions with the regulators. If you ever receive different advice than this, please get a second opinion before making any commitments.

Assuming an organization decides to pursue a captive because operating a legitimate insurance company makes good business sense, the organization has passed the first hurdle to deductibility: a valid purpose for existence. If a captive exists for no other valid purpose than tax benefits, then no other analysis matters—deductibility will be challenged.

How to qualify as a legitimate insurance company for tax purposes has been the subject of significant judicial and regulatory activity. As far as the IRS is concerned, just calling your organization an insurance company doesn't make it one. In fact, a company that has a license to operate as an insurance company in a particular jurisdiction isn't automatically qualified as an insurance company for tax treatment according to the IRS (and the judicial system). Decisions from the appellate courts have made it clear that the term "insurance" is a term of art that has been given a specific legal meaning. Simply stated, if your organization does not meet certain requirements then it will not be considered an insurance company for tax purposes; to be sure, many captives fail to meet the required qualifications without ever realizing it. And when they find out, the lesson is a financially painful one.

What is "insurance"?
I will try to stay at a 10,000 foot level when discussing the tax aspects of a captive insurance company. The laws surrounding the tax treatment of captive insurance companies is complex and must be dealt with by a qualified advisor. In order to be considered insurance, a company must purchase it from an insurance company.

Essentially, the IRS has said that for an arrangement to be considered "insurance" for Federal income tax purposes risk shifting *and* risk distribution must exist. Shifting means you have moved the risk off your books and given it to a separate entity. According to the Financial Accounting Standards (FAS) a company that is selfinsured has to account for liabilities. This often creates problems and confusion with many business owners. The business has to deduct these reserves for financial reporting, but they can not take a deduction for tax-purposes. Self-insured losses are only deductible for tax purposes when the losses are incurred and paid.

This is clearly an example of risk that is not shifted to any other entity. The more difficult discussion is the distribution of risk once it is shifted to that separate entity.

FAS 113

In order for a policy to be considered "insurance," the Financial Accounting Standard 113 requires there must be a chance of underwriting loss. Investment risk and timing risk alone will not constitute an insurance contract. When designing insurance contracts to be issued by a captive, the actuaries use an industry rule of thumb: in order to qualify as insurance, there must be a 10% chance of a 10% loss.

FAS 113 also sets guidelines for the other rules of thumb tests the IRS should use in determining if insurance exists. The first rule the IRS will use in determining if insurance exists is whether or not the event being insured has already occurred. You can buy insurance to cover some prior acts, but to be considered insurance the losses can not be known to the insurer at the time the policy is issued.

A second rule of thumb for insurance is whether or not there is a reasonable chance the insurance company will have a loss on a policy. In my opinion, this is the art and science of creating insurance contracts. The goal of an insurance company is to write a policy broad enough to qualify as insurance, but narrow enough (and with enough exclusions) to prevent losses for every claim under the sun.

A simple example I use in practice is this: Insurance company ABC can write an auto insurance policy that will cover accidents for a driver at any point. That is clearly an insurance contract. If the carrier re-wrote the policy so the insuring agreement said it would only be liable for an accident that occurred on a specific freeway, on a Sunday afternoon between 4:00 p.m. and 6:00 p.m., that is *not* insurance. Although there is such an actuarial probability of that occurring, this is not reasonable. That brings us back to the 10% chance of a 10% loss test.

Just because a captive is considered an insurance company does NOT mean the premiums are deductible to the corporation. But if the captive is not an insurance company for tax purposes, the premiums are guaranteed NOT to be deductible. In order to take a deduction the IRS has established clear guidelines of how to qualify as an insurance company and how the policies written can be valid insurance contracts, i.e. deductible for tax purposes.

This was specifically addressed by the IRS in its Revenue Ruling 2005-40, released in July 2005. In the ruling, the IRS addressed the issue of whether certain circumstances constitute an insurance arrangement for federal income tax purposes and whether the issuer qualifies as an insurance company for federal income tax purposes.

In its ruling, the IRS wrote:

> In order to determine the nature of an arrangement for federal income tax purposes, it is necessary to consider all the facts and circumstances in a particular case, including not only the terms of the arrangement, but also the entire course of conduct of the parties. Thus, an arrangement that purports to be an insurance contract but lacks the requisite risk distribution may instead be characterized as a deposit arrange-

ment, a loan, a contribution to capital (to the extent of net value, if any), an indemnity arrangement that is not an insurance contract, or otherwise, based on the substance of the arrangement between the parties. The proper characterization of the arrangement may determine whether the issuer qualifies as an insurance company and whether amounts paid under the arrangement may be deductible.[ix]

The ruling then went on to more specifically address "risk distribution" and "risk shifting."

Risk shifting occurs if a person facing the possibility of an economic loss transfers some or all of the financial consequences of the potential loss to the insurer, such that a loss by the insured does not affect the insured because the loss is offset by a payment from the insurer.[x]

Citing *Clougherty Packing Co. v. Commissioner*,[xi] the ruling noted,

Risk distribution incorporates the statistical phenomenon known as the law of large numbers. Distributing risk allows the insurer to reduce the possibility that a single costly claim will exceed the amount taken in as premiums and set aside for the payment of such a claim. By assuming numerous relatively small, independent risks that occur randomly over time, the insurer smoothes out losses to match more closely its receipt of premiums.[xii]

The ruling presented how a few courts have defined "risk distribution":

Courts have recognized that risk distribution necessarily entails a pooling of premiums, so that a potential insured is not in significant part paying for its own risks. Humana, Inc. v. Commissioner, 881 F.2d 247, 257 (6th Cir. 1989). See also Ocean Drilling & Exploration Co. v. United States, 988 F.2d

1135, 1153 (Fed. Cir. 1993) ("Risk distribution involves spreading the risk of loss among policyholders."); Beech Aircraft Corp. v. United States, 797 F.2d 920, 922 (10th Cir. 1986) ("'[R]isk distributing' means that the party assuming the risk distributes his potential liability, in part, among others."); Treganowan, at 291 (quoting Note, The New York Stock Exchange Gratuity Fund: Insurance that Isn't Insurance, 59 Yale L. J. 780, 784 (1950)) ("By diffusing the risks through a mass of separate risk shifting contracts, the insurer casts his lot with the law of averages. The process of risk distribution, therefore, is the very essence of insurance."); Crawford Fitting Co. v. United States, 606 F. Supp. 136, 147 (N.D. Ohio 1985) ("[T]he court finds . . . that various non-affiliated persons or entities facing risks similar but independent of those faced by plaintiff were named insureds under the policy, enabling the distribution of the risk thereunder."); AMERCO and Subsidiaries v. Commissioner, 96 T.C. 18, 41 (1991), aff'd, 979 F.2d 162 (9th Cir. 1992) ("The concept of risk-distributing emphasizes the pooling aspect of insurance: that it is the nature of an insurance contract to be part of a larger collection of coverages, combined to distribute risk between insureds.").[xiii]

The IRS illustrated its ruling by considering four circumstances in which certain arrangements between unrelated entities do and do not constitute insurance for federal income tax purposes.

Situation 1
- X owns and operates a large fleet of vehicles
- Vehicles represent a significant volume of independent, "homogeneous" risk
- X enters into an arrangement with unrelated Y where in exchange for "premiums", Y agrees to "insure" X against risk of loss with respect to X's vehicle fleet
- Y does not "insure" any entity other than X

100%
Premiums

Corporation X
(U.S. Domiciled)

Corporation Y
(U.S. Domiciled)

Risk Funding
Contract

(Y insures risks
of X only)

Situation 2

- Same as Situation 1, except that Y also "insures" unrelated Z in exchange for "premiums against risk of loss with respect to Z's vehicle fleet in the conduct of a business substantially similar to that of X
- Y's earnings from its arrangement with Z constitute 10% of Y's total amount earned (both gross and net) during the year and the risk exposure attributable to Z comprise 10% of the total risk borne by Y

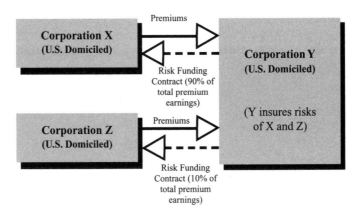

Premiums

Corporation X
(U.S. Domiciled)

Corporation Y
(U.S. Domiciled)

Risk Funding
Contract (90% of
total premium
earnings)

Premiums

Corporation Z
(U.S. Domiciled)

(Y insures risks
of X and Z)

Risk Funding
Contract (10% of
total premium
earnings)

Situation 3

X conducts a courier business through 12 LLCs that are disregarded entities for Federal income tax purposes.

The LLCs own a fleet of vehicles that represent a significant volume of independent, homogeneous risk;

Each of the LLCs enters into an arrangement with Y where unrelated Y agrees to "insure" the LLC against risk of loss with respect to its vehicle fleet;

Y does not "insure" any entity other than the LLCs; and

None of the LLCs account for less than 5%, or more than 15% of the total risk assumed by Y.

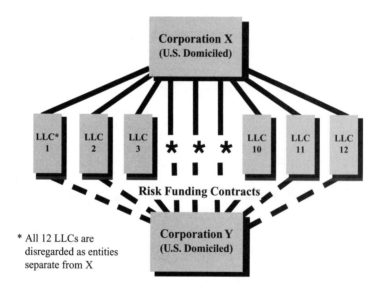

Situation 4

Same as Situation 3, except that the 12 LLCs elect to be treated as corporations for Federal income tax purposes.

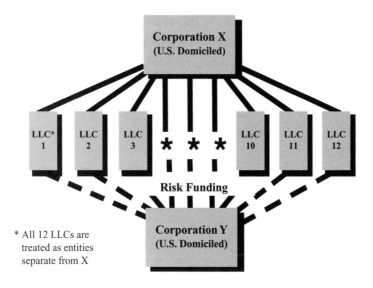

* All 12 LLCs are treated as entities separate from X

IRS Ruling 2005–40 Holding

The IRS concluded situations 1, 2 and 3 did not constitute insurance for Federal income tax purposes. It concluded that situation 4 however, did constitute insurance for Federal income tax purposes and the issuer did qualify as an insurance company. In this scenario, the IRS concluded that the amounts paid to the issuer were deductible as insurance premiums under section 162 of the Internal Revenue Code.

Why is this ruling so important?

This ruling is important for those operating a captive insurance company (or considering it) because it provides relatively clear guidance regarding the two elements that the IRS currently believes are necessary to achieve appropriate risk distribution:

- First, in order for the law of large numbers to take effect, a significant number of "independent, homogeneous risks" must be transferred to the captive.
- Second, the risk that the captive is underwriting must come from several entities that are "independent" (from the perspective of Federal income tax).

So a captive that intends to insure the risks of only the parent will not be considered an insurance company for Federal income tax purposes because there is no independent homogenous risk from several different independent entities.

If you are a captive or are considering establishing a captive, you want to know what you can do to establish risk distribution that passes IRS scrutiny; there are two prominent methods: underwriting an appropriate percentage of unrelated risk or as we saw in situation 4 of Revenue Ruling 2005-40, underwriting the risk of 11 or more organizations that are not disregarded for Federal income tax purposes.

Safe harbors
Unrelated risk - The first safe harbor involves writing insurance that is unrelated to the owner (unrelated third parties). The amount of insurance that must be written isn't completely clear but most experts agree that if the captive is writing at least 50% unrelated risk the IRS will be satisfied.

About now, you might be thinking: "Fifty percent! I'm not setting up a captive to underwrite the risk of unaffiliated third parties! Even if I wanted to, how would I do that?"

That reaction would be understandable. But remember, to the IRS, if you are claiming to be an insurance company then you should operate like one. And in reality, this isn't quite as challenging as it might seem. Most captives qualify for insurance-company tax treatment using this safe harbor. Typically, the captive's management company or consultants assist in securing reinsurance from third parties that meets these requirements.

One of the most common ways to achieve risk distribution and unrelated risk is through the use of a risk pool. These pools are commonly referred to as retrocessional risk pools. In these pools, a portion of the entire premium written by the pool is given back or retroceeded to all of the captive participants. The captive pays a premium to the pool for the pool to take some of its risk. The captive then reinsures the risk pool for a percentage of all of the risk or the pool. When the captive reinsures the pool it receives premiums from the pool adequate for the risk exposure.

Figure 6.1 - Retrocessional risk pools

Retrocessional Risk Pools

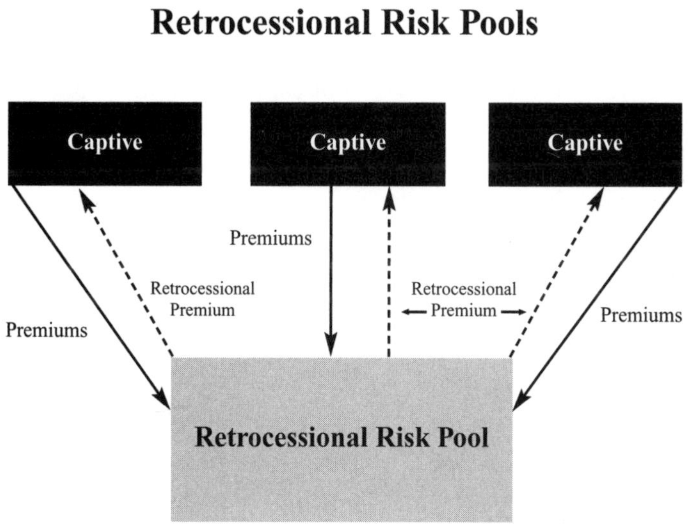

By participating in a risk pool, a single parent captive owner that has one entity has the ability to create legitimate risk distribution. Caution must be taken to make sure the risk pool operates with strict underwriting and admission criteria. A few bad risks can torpedo the benefits of a captive insurance company.

Eleven or more insureds - If you are still not comfortable underwriting 50% unrelated third-party risk, you could consider this safe harbor. As outlined by the IRS in Revenue Ruling 2005-40, this insurance arrangement requires the captive to underwrite the risk of eleven or more entities that are not disregarded for Federal income tax purposes.

This will not be possible for many organizations, but for some, it is a perfect fit. For example, we have helped many contractor clients use this safe harbor effectively. Essentially, our clients will set up a legal entity (e.g., a limited liability company) for each major construction project. The captive then underwrites risks of each LLC; if there are not at least 11 such organizations, then the captive meets the IRS requirements.

Different issues and types of captives
All of the preceding information was to set the stage for my basic philosophy on captives and tax treatment of the various entities. There are a few types of captives and the subtle differences should be addressed. We will discuss 3 types of tax treatment for captives: the 501(c)(15), the 831(b) and a regular captive insurance company.

IRC Section 501(c)(15) captives
The 501(c)(15) provision is of limited value to captive operators today. When it was initially enacted it provided an avenue for a specific type of insurance company to operate tax free. After a series of abuses, the provision was amended to provide that a property and casualty insurance company is eligible to be exempt from federal income tax only if gross receipts for the taxable year do not exceed $600,000 and more than 50 percent of such gross receipts consist of premiums; effectively, this limited tax free investment income to no more than $300,000 per year.[xiv]

This structure was also added to the IRS list of "listed transactions." If you choose to operate under 501(c)(15), you are required to file a form notifying the IRS that you are pursuing something they told you they don't like. It doesn't mean your premiums will be denied, but no business owner needs that kind of hassle.

IRC Section 831(b) Election
Internal Revenue Code §831(b) offers small insurance compa-

nies a very powerful tax advantage that can provide financial resources to pay claims. This benefit assumes that legitimate risk is being transferred. It is available to both onshore and offshore captives. This election makes the premiums paid to the captive not subject to income taxes. The reserves are accumulated, and the insurance company is only taxed on its investment income. The application of the 831(b) election is straightforward. Any properly structured insurance captive writing less than $1.2 million of annual premium may take this election.

IRC 831(b) allows for a property and casualty company to be taxed only on its investment income. The advantage of this structure is that it allows the company to accumulate surplus from underwriting profits free from tax. However, it is important to note that while an 831(b) pays no tax on underwriting profit, its owners are still taxed on dividends and other compensation received.

An 831(b) insurance company has become a popular structure for captive promoters, and I have found the basic sales pitch is "how would you like to deduct $1.2 million and ultimately pay capital gains on the distribution?" Let me say this is dangerous and I will revisit this topic after my discussion of non-831(b) insurance companies below.

Regular property/casualty companies
If a captive insurance company receives more than $1.2 million in premiums or has not elected 831(b) insurance taxation, it is considered a "regular" captive insurance company. To review, the 831(b) company will enjoy tax-free premiums and tax liability on only the investment growth. A regular property-casualty company does not have the same tax treatment.

Non-831(b) companies are taxed on the premium income received. But they are afforded a deduction for legitimate reserves, incurred- but-not-reported ("IBNR") losses, expenses, reinsurance, claims, etc. So, the non-831(b) company can still

avoid paying taxes in circumstances where its approved deductions offset premium income. For example, even though a
captive charges $5 million in premiums, it will pay no taxes if
it has $500,000 in expenses and IBNR and can actuarially jus-
tify reserves of $4.5 million.

In analyzing whether a captive makes sense, the manager and
actuary should look at the amount of coverage and reinsurance
costs, when the claims are likely to happen, and the interest
rate (or discount factor) applied to the loss reserves.

The taxation of insurance companies is unique among companies in other U.S. industries—and for good reason. Most of our
clients are business owners who manufacture a product. They
buy raw materials, manufacture a product, sell the product and
get paid. The income on which they are taxed, is based on the
difference between the revenue from selling their products and
the expenses incurred to achieve those sales. If the IRS made
insurance companies use that same rationale, the income that
would have to be reported would have relatively little expense
to offset it; this is because the approach wouldn't recognize the
fact that a large portion of the claims against which the income
would be offset don't occur until future years.

Depending on timing, a captive may not be an appropriate vehicle. For example, we occasionally advise companies who
currently self insure that if most of their claims are paid in the
year they occur, a captive provides little arbitrage for them.
The captive makes the most sense when premium is paid, and
claims are uncertain and are often paid out after many years.
Here, a captive is an appropriate choice.

Problems/potential issues
I have seen many captive-promoter proposals that manufacture
polices and risks. The predominate structure I see is the 831(b)
captive. A reason for this is the ability to justify low reserves
in the company. If the company were to pay $1,000,000 in pre-

miums into a non-831(b) where only $500,000 was necessary, the captive would be faced with taxable income of $500,000. If the captive were structured under 831(b), the company would only pay taxes on the investment earnings.

As you might guess, there is a whole host of problems when captives are being pitched as a tax dodge. In its simplest form, all insurance companies, captives and otherwise get a deduction today to fund reserves necessary in the future. With an 831(b) there is not as much of a need to keep the reserves close to the premium. To illustrate the point, a company pays $1,200,000 in premium (lets call it terrorism insurance), the actuarial study represents the client only needs $400,000 for reserves. In a non-831(b) company, there would be a large tax bill, in the 831(b) there would not. The IRS could take the position, If you only needed $400,000 to fully fund reserves, the excess premiums were an unnecessary business expense.

This is just a word of caution; I do not mean to imply all 831(b)'s are bad; there are legitimate reasons to form a captive under this provision. However, I would urge you to have the insurance company taxation analysis completed as if it were *not* an 831(b) so you can clearly see the advantages of operating as an 831(b) captive. I believe 831(b) captives will come under attack from the IRS at some point, so in most cases whether a client puts in $750,000, $1.2 million or $2 million, I often recommend not taking the 831(b) election. Captive insurance companies that do not take this election tend to look, act, and smell like traditional insurance companies. They may ultimately pay more in taxes, but everyone associated with them sleeps better at night.

As should be clear from this discussion, understanding the tax implications of operating a captive insurance company is of significant importance. Although tax impact can be a valuable asset if the captive is appropriately structured, it can also create a very difficult and expensive set of challenges if mishandled. As always, it is best to retain tax advice from qualified tax professionals with a strong background in the intricacies of captive insurance companies.

Chapter 7: What are the risks associated with forming and operating a captive?

So far, we've talked about the many advantages of forming a captive insurance company. We've addressed some traditional uses of a captive, how to establish a captive and some of the advantages from a tax perspective. But there is another side of the captive story that needs to be understood as a part of the due diligence process: the risks of forming and operating a captive.

For so many reasons, a captive model has become a mainstream option for companies of all sizes. But it has not always been that way. As we discussed previously, most jurisdictions did not recognize captives as legitimate insurance companies in the early years. For the trailblazers, captive formation meant going offshore. And going offshore meant an increased skepticism of the legitimacy of an organization's risk-financing strategies. With increased skepticism came increased scrutiny. And often, increased scrutiny resulted in government action with negative financial consequences. But hey, that was then, this is now—things are completely different today, right?

Well, yes and no. There is no question that the most popular captive structures of today are now well-accepted risk financing tools. But that doesn't mean that they are always used properly. In addition, just because there is a well-accepted, legitimate captive industry that is part of the mainstream, doesn't mean there aren't highly risky structures that masquerade as legitimate captives. Understanding what to look for (and what to look out for!) is critical for anyone considering forming a captive.

From a broad view of the questionable structures, there are three areas to consider:

1) those that write only uninsured risk;
2) those that are simply of unsound design and often the result of questionable marketing practices; and
3) those that form without ensuring they meet relevant IRS safe harbor provisions.

We'll address each category individually and then discuss a few other areas of potential risk.

Those that write only uninsured risk
One of the reasons I wrote this book was my belief there were abuses in the captive insurance marketplace. As with most industries, there are many true professionals and a few that are not so professional. Captive legislation was created on a federal level to allow businesses to escape the market cycles of the insurance industry. That was the purpose and if used correctly, there is nothing better. All businesses have risk they have insured and some risk they have self insured (either consciously or unconsciously). Many of the captive proposals we run across involve businesses that simply design policies to cover uninsured risk. They will go into a business and ask how large of a deduction they would like and they try to come up with risks and polices to validate the (usually) $1,200,000 de-

duction. The issue with this type of planning is that it ignores the reasonableness test of the insurance. Let me give you an example.

We were recently hired by a law firm to analyze a captive proposal presented to one of its clients by a captive promoter. The proposal involved the firm's client—a small company in a small town—taking a $1,200,000 deduction to provide terrorism insurance to small manufacturers. Despite the fact that the model looked to be perfect in every aspect of the formation, something didn't seem right to the attorneys.

As we reviewed the plan, it appeared the captive promoter thought through every detail and IRS regulation. It was to be domiciled offshore and was structured to take a section 953(d) election. They had actuarial report after report to support their position. In fact, the promoter was adamant that the captive would pass any IRS scrutiny should it choose to send an agent to the British Virgin Islands to kick some tires. We agreed—except on one point. The promoter overlooked a very important issue. This company could have purchased a commercially available policy (if they desired) for under $10,000!

The IRS is very astute when it comes to the design and implementation of captives. In this case, they would quickly deny the proposed deduction under section 162 "Ordinary and *necessary*" business expense" (emphasis supplied). This policy had not been necessary for the company's prior thirty years in business. If there was a legitimate need for this type of coverage, the insured would have to demonstrate that something must have changed to warrant its necessity. Not surprisingly, no such necessity existed.

We have seen dozens and dozens of examples of such questionable strategies. One of my favorites has to be the captive created by an anesthesiologist with two employees. His captive was formed for the specific purpose of providing him with sexual harassment coverage. The premium cost $1,200,000 annually.

As pointed out throughout this book, a captive must look, act and smell like an insurance company providing legitimate coverage. That is the only way a business owner should expect a premium to pass scrutiny with the IRS. So how do you decide what's legitimate? We begin with the premiums and coverages a client purchases every day. There are often limitations to such coverages that can be better designed by the client. Obviously, if you have been purchasing the coverage from the traditional insurance market, there exists a presumption of necessity. If the captive can tailor the coverage to more effectively meet your needs, then the IRS will be hard pressed to argue the policy is not legitimate.

Unsound design and questionable marketing practices
One of the risks to be aware of today is the aggressively promoted strategy trying to convince you it is the greatest tax avoidance program in existence. I have personally witnessed too much of this. It is not only a risk to those who buy-in; it is a risk to the entire industry. Poorly conceived structures that do not have legitimate insurance purposes should be avoided at all costs. Always remember to carefully analyze the background and credentials of the service providers with whom you are working. You can learn a lot from a person's background. For example, there are many promoters who advertise "we are not property/casualty insurance agents." They actually present this as a strength claiming that it would be a conflict of interest to sell PC insurance and market captive structures. I vigorously disagree. I have yet to figure out how someone can set up and understand captive insurance companies and how risk functions in the marketplace without being PC licensed. Moreover, anyone setting up a captive needs to clearly understand the property/casualty industry if they are to be effective at all in designing policies that will accomplish what the business owner wants and needs.

It can't be repeated often enough: It is vital for clients to be educated on captives because many promoters leave out the important details. Not all do it intentionally; they simply may not know the details. And while it would be easy at this point to broadly criticize captive promoters, this space is better allocated to discussing some specific issues related to captive formation and structure strategy.

Consider, for example, segregated cell captives. As discussed in chapter 3, a cell captive allows other captives to be formed underneath it. Every cell captive is supposed to be a standalone entity. Some promoters take the position that each cell does not have to have risk distribution or shifting because the parent captive has enough cells to create enough risk distribution and shifting overall. While it is true (as of the publication date of this book at least) that the IRS has not litigated this position, I believe the IRS will eventually take the position that every cell must have distribution and shifting. A smart captive owner structures for the long term and understands where taking risks with the structure are not prudent.

Many promoters use captives as a thinly veiled attempt to sell life insurance to prospects. Although there are some phenomenal benefits and reasons to purchase insurance inside of the captive, this should not be marketed as a way to sell life insurance on a deductible basis. The IRS has systematically eliminated or reduced the impact of many of the strategies used by life insurance agents to generate large deductions or sell large premiums. These include section 79 group term life insurance, multiple employer welfare benefit plans (§419A(f)6 plans), §412(i) plans, deferred compensation plans and non-recourse premium financing. I have seen a proposal that described Captives as "Tax-deductible, discriminatory, deferred compensation." Those who are enticed by such dubious marketing find themselves stepping out onto a slippery slope that often lands them upside down. In the end, bad captive structures—and those who market them—cast a negative light on the entire industry. Because of this, it is more important than ever to make sure if the IRS looks closely at this, your captive is on firm footing.

Failing to meet relevant IRS safe harbor provisions

Revenue ruling 2005-40 is the IRS' attempt to outline what is acceptable. We have discussed the ruling earlier, but it bears repeating. The ruling illustrates four situations the IRS considers acceptable practice. If you stay within the safe harbor, you do not need a private letter ruling. Here are the scenarios as presented in the revenue ruling (in an attempt to add clarity, the revenue ruling has been re-ordered for the reader):

Situation 1 X, a domestic corporation, operates a courier transport business covering a large portion of the United States. X owns and operates a large fleet of automotive vehicles representing a significant volume of independent, homogeneous risks. For valid, non-tax business purposes, X entered into an arrangement with Y, an unrelated domestic corporation, whereby in exchange for an agreed amount of "premiums," Y "insures" X against the risk of loss arising out of the operation of its fleet in the conduct of its courier business.

The amount of "premiums" under the arrangement is determined at arm's length according to customary insurance industry rating formulas. Y possesses adequate capital to fulfill its obligations to X under the agreement, and in all respects operates in accordance with the applicable requirements of state law. There are no guarantees of any kind in favor of Y with respect to the agreement, nor are any of the "premiums" paid by X to Y in turn loaned back to X. X has no obligation to pay Y additional premiums if X's actual losses during any period of coverage exceed the "premiums" paid by X. X will not be entitled to any refund of "premiums" paid if X's actual losses are lower than the "premiums" paid during any period. In all respects, the parties conduct themselves con-

sistent with the standards applicable to an insurance arrangement between unrelated parties, except that Y does not "insure" any entity other than X.

Analysis

In order to determine the nature of an arrangement for federal income tax purposes, it is necessary to consider all the
facts and circumstances in a particular case, including not
only the terms of the arrangement, but also the entire course
of conduct of the parties. Thus, an arrangement that purports
to be an insurance contract but lacks the requisite risk distribution may instead be characterized as a deposit arrangement, a loan, a contribution to capital (to the extent of net
value, if any), an indemnity arrangement that is not an insurance contract, or otherwise, based on the substance of the
arrangement between the parties. The proper characterization of the arrangement may determine whether the issuer
qualifies as an insurance company and whether amounts paid
under the arrangement may be deductible.

In Situation 1, Y enters into an "insurance" arrangement with
X. The arrangement with X represents Y's only such agreement. Although the arrangement may shift the risks of X to
Y, those risks are not, in turn, distributed among other insureds or policyholders. Therefore, the arrangement between
X and Y does not constitute insurance for federal income tax
purposes.

Situation 2 The facts are the same as in Situation 1 except
that, in addition to its arrangement with X, Y enters into an
arrangement with Z, a domestic corporation unrelated to X
or Y, whereby in exchange for an agreed amount of "premiums," Y also "insures" Z against the risk of loss arising out
of the operation of its own fleet in connection with the conduct of a courier business substantially similar to that of X.
The amounts Y earns from its arrangements with Z constitute
10% of Y's total amounts earned during the taxable year on

both a gross and net basis. The arrangement with Z accounts for 10% of the total risks borne by Y.

Analysis

In Situation 2, the fact that Y also enters into an arrangement with Z does not change the conclusion that the arrangement between X and Y lacks the requisite risk distribution to constitute insurance. Y's contract with Z represents only 10% of the total amounts earned by Y, and 10% of total risks assumed, under all its arrangements. This creates an insufficient pool of other premiums to distribute X's risk. See Rev. Rul. 2002-89, 2002-2 C.B. 984 (concluding that risks from unrelated parties representing 10% of total risks borne by subsidiary are insufficient to qualify arrangement between parent and subsidiary as insurance).

Situation 3 X, a domestic corporation, operates a courier transport business covering a large portion of the United States. X conducts the courier transport business through 12 limited liability companies (LLCs) of which it is the single member. The LLCs are disregarded as entities separate from X under the provisions of §301.7701-3 of the Procedure and Administration Regulations. The LLCs own and operate a large fleet of automotive vehicles, collectively representing a significant volume of independent, homogeneous risks. For valid, non-tax business purposes, the LLCs entered into arrangements with Y, an unrelated domestic corporation, whereby in exchange for an agreed amount of "premiums," Y "insures" the LLCs against the risk of loss arising out of the operation of the fleet in the conduct of their courier business. None of the LLCs account for less than 5%, or more than 15%, of the total risk assumed by Y under the agreements.

The amount of "premiums" under the arrangement is determined at arm's length according to customary insurance industry rating formulas. Y possesses adequate capital to fulfill its obligations to the LLCs under the agreement, and in all respects operates in accordance with the licensing and other requirements of state law. There are no guarantees of any kind in favor of Y with respect to the agreements, nor are any of the "premiums" paid by the LLCs to Y in turn loaned back to X or to the LLCs. No LLC has any obligation to pay Y additional premiums if that LLC's actual losses during the arrangement exceed the "premiums" paid by that LLC. No LLC will be entitled to a refund of "premiums" paid if that LLC's actual losses are lower than the "premiums" paid during any period. Y retains the risks that it assumes under the agreement. In all respects, the parties conduct themselves consistent with the standards applicable to an insurance arrangement between unrelated parties, except that Y does not "insure" any entity other than the LLCs.

Analysis

In Situation 3, Y contracts only with 12 single member LLCs through which X conducts a courier transport business. The LLCs are disregarded as entities separate from X pursuant to § 301.7701-3. Section 301.7701-2(a) provides that if an entity is disregarded, its activities are treated in the same manner as a sole proprietorship, branch or division of the owner. Applying this rule in Situation 3, Y has entered into an "insurance" arrangement only with X. Therefore, for the reasons set forth in Situation 1 above, the arrangement between X and Y does not constitute insurance for federal income tax purposes.

Situation 4 The facts are the same as in Situation 3, except that each of the 12 LLCs elects pursuant to § 301.7701-3(a) to be classified as an association.

Analysis

In Situation 4, the 12 LLCs are not disregarded as entities separate from X, but instead are classified as associations for federal income tax purposes. The arrangements between

Y and each LLC thus shift a risk of loss from each LLC to Y. The risks of the LLCs are distributed among the various other LLCs that are insured under similar arrangements. Therefore the arrangements between the 12 LLCs and Y constitute insurance for federal income tax purposes. See Rev. Rul. 2002-90, 2002-2 C.B. 985 (similar arrangements between affiliated entities constituted insurance). Because the arrangements with the 12 LLCs represent Y's only business, and those arrangements are insurance contracts for federal income tax purposes, Y is an insurance company within the meaning of §§ 831(c) and 816(a). In addition, the 12 LLCs may be entitled to deduct amounts paid under those arrangements as insurance premiums under §162 if the requirements for deduction are otherwise satisfied.

Law
See Appendix B for a discussion of relevant law under Rev. Ruling 2005-40.

Holdings
In Situations 1, 2 and 3, the arrangements do not constitute insurance for federal income tax purposes. In Situation 4, the arrangements constitute insurance for federal income tax purposes and the issuer qualifies as an insurance company. The amounts paid to the issuer may be deductible as insurance premiums under §162 if the requirements for deduction are otherwise satisfied.[xv]

As you can see from the IRS analysis above, time spent carefully structuring your captive is time well spent. And while we'd all love to believe that the IRS position on these issues is set in stone, the reality is that the only thing we can count on is constant change. The IRS has a long history of interpreting and re-interpreting tax laws. Although captives are (or should be) set up for non-tax benefits, the taxation cannot be ignored. The IRS chooses its battles carefully and those they choose they pursue vigorously. Because of the ever changing nature of tax codes it is important to have competent advisors to help you in this area. Those who expect there will be changes to tax law and accept that they need appropriate advisors on their team to keep them up to date on the changes and offering advice on how and when to respond to such changes are putting themselves in the best position.

Unfortunately, there is simply nothing any one company can do about changes in tax law. What they can do, however, is understand the relevant code, use competent advisors to plan accordingly and structure conservatively. This strategy has proven to be the best for those who don't like surprises and who prefer reasonable levels of predictability.

Additional areas of potential risk

In addition to the three areas we just reviewed, there are two other potential risk areas to consider:

- The risk inherent in the reinsurance market and
- The risk of poor captive management

Reinsurance market

Traditional coverage and reinsurance are closely related. If reinsurers experience a catastrophic event such as hurricane Katrina, they will need to increase their rates. If they increase the rates to traditional carriers, those carriers have a few options. They can in turn increase their rates, or keep their premiums the same and take on more liability per claim. Most insurance decisions made by traditional carriers involve the profitability to the shareholders. If there is a likelihood of loss, the traditional carrier will be unlikely to retain more risk. They are likely to increase the premiums they charge their policy holders. Conversely, if premiums in the traditional markets are falling, it is very likely—if not certain—the underlying cost of reinsurance has fallen.

It is the uncertainty within the reinsurance market that creates risk. Nevertheless, financially strong companies with good risk management practices are likely to benefit from negotiating a strong reinsurance treaty in both soft and hard markets. We have recently had success in negotiating multi-year coverage for many captives. With good claims experience, they will not have to renegotiate reinsurance for a 3-5 year time frame.

Captive Insight

For more information about reinsurance, log on to www.TakenCaptive.com and enter the word: "reinsurance" in the "**Captive Insight**" box.

Poor captive management

A captive is a complex vehicle and the captive manager is at the center of it. Although a careful structure and business plan go a long way to minimizing risk, the captive manager must be effective in order for the captive to be effective. A competent captive manager is akin to having a skilled quarterback. The game plan may be sound, but it still must be executed and a disproportionate amount of the responsibility lies in the hands of the quarterback. The captive manager is the captive owner's eyes and ears in the domicile. The risks are great because the manager oversees the policy writing, taxation, accounting, underwriting, regulatory changes and board member communications. If the manager loses focus the risk of loss to the owner can be substantial. The most prominent risk is compliance. If the captive is not compliant in the domicile, the ability to write insurance can go away quickly. A captive that is out of compliance is no longer an insurance company. That not only means an inability to write insurance, it also means an inability to use insurance company taxation treatment. Financially, this is obviously a significant risk.

This discussion of potential risks should underscore the importance of careful attention to the details of structure and formation. When you understand where companies can easily jump the track, you are better prepared to get it right the first time. In the next chapter, we take a closer look at the formation process.

Chapter 8: What are the steps involved in forming a captive?

When a company contemplates the formation of a captive insurance company as a part of its risk-financing strategy, it typically conducts a feasibility study. The feasibility study is actually quite often a requirement by domiciles but that should not be the sole reason it is conducted. The critical purpose of a feasibility study is to evaluate the efficacy of the captive investment. That is, the study answers the question, "What can I expect as a return on my investment in this captive insurance company?" While an investment in a captive is not the same as an investment in a new piece of business-related equipment or an investment in a new start-up division of the company, it none the less will have a financial impact that must be clearly evaluated and understood prior to formation. Because of the distinct differences between analyzing a captive insurance company investment and a more typical investment related to the business operations, it's crucially important to involve risk-management advisors who are experienced in performing captive-feasibility studies. We will address the specific components of a feasibility study in chapter 8.

When the feasibility study reveals that a captive insurance company will provide appropriate investment returns for the captive investor(s) (and keep in mind that "appropriate return" does not always mean a direct financial profit), the formation process becomes a reality and the more detailed operational analysis begins (see Appendix C for a sample timeline of all the major components of captive formation). Often, the initial step is writing the business plan for the captive insurance company. A company or group who decides to form an insurance company should never do so without a business plan. Like the feasibility study, a business plan is sometimes required by domiciles; but also like the feasibility study, domicile requirement should not be the incentive for writing one.

Forming a captive should receive the same attention as forming any new company. In fact, it might even require greater attention than some startups, given the regulatory oversight. That means that developing a business plan for the company should be considered a critical tool for the success of the captive.

Captive Insight

Captive business plans come in many forms. To see a sample captive business plan, go to www.takencaptive.com and enter the phrase: "Business Plan" in the "Captive Insight" box.

The business plan will help the captive owner clearly articulate the captive's business profile. This is important for determining the most appropriate uses of the captive and the impact of the captive on the parent's business model. This is also an important tool for use in defining the most appropriate domicile.

Components of a captive business plan

A captive business plan will have many of the elements of a traditional business plan such as company overview, identification of the captive's ownership structure, capitalization and organizational structure; but there will also be distinct differences. The captive business plan will also include a discussion of coverages and coverage limits the captive will offer, a discussion of the captive governance profile and a relatively detailed review of the captive's operations plan.

The captive's financials will be covered in detail and will include such components as the captive's underwriting policy, surplus contribution and withdrawal policy, loss-control process and claims-handling procedures. The business plan will also cover the captive's reinsurance plan.

Many business plans will include, as attachments, articles of incorporation, bylaws, organizational charts (including outsourced partners), the feasibility study and actuarial reports with projections of expected losses.

Domicile formation requirements

After the feasibility study and business planning is completed and the captive investor is convinced that operating a captive still makes sense, it's time to begin reviewing in greater detail the formation requirements of the captive's potential domicile(s).

The process will differ depending on the captive structure and the domicile that is selected, but, for the most part, the elements are consistent:

1. Contact the domicile to obtain latest formation requirements (At this point, some domiciles will request/expect a meeting with appropriate insurance department personnel to learn about the proposed captive and its goals)

2. Complete and submit the license application

3. Complete corporate formation within the domicile

4. Timely respond to supplemental information requests

5. Captive is formed and formal regulatory oversight practices are implemented

One of the best ways to understand specifically what domiciles expect is to see their exact requirements. Below, we've presented Vermont's and New York's formation requirements.

Steps to form a captive in Vermont

The following is reproduced from the Vermont captive industry's Website: www.VermontCaptive.com. It is presented as a current example of what to expect in terms of forming a captive in a popular U.S. domicile.

"Generally, the process of incorporating a captive insurer in Vermont and applying for a license from the Department of Banking, Insurance, Securities and Health Care Administration will involve the following steps:

Call or E-mail us to arrange a meeting with the Deputy Commissioner of Captive Insurance and staff to discuss the proposed captive and obtain initial reactions from the Department.

Prepare documents necessary for incorporation. The services of a local lawyer may be desirable.

Prepare documents necessary for application to the Department (See captive application for a list of these items.)

Submit one copy of all materials in numbers (2) and (3) above to the Commissioner of Banking, Insurance, Securities and Health Care Administration for review. Include a $200.00 application fee and $4,000.00 review firm fee.

Submit one additional copy of the application material to the assigned review firm when instructed to do so by the Commissioner.

Petition the Commissioner to issue a Certificate of Public

Good. The factors to be addressed are outlined in 8 V.S.A. Sec 6006(d).

After the Commissioner has issued the Certificate of Public Good, present this and the documents in number (2) above to the Secretary of State's office along with the appropriate fee in order to incorporate the captive (see 11 V.S.A. Sec 2201).

After the incorporation, apply to the Commissioner for a Certificate of Authority and submit a $300.00 license fee."[xvi]

Vermont identifies the following items as "other requirements."

1. Select a Vermont approved management firm

2. Have your CPA complete the necessary form for authorization to perform audits.

3. Have your actuary complete the necessary form for authorization to render the opinion on reserves.

4. An organizational exam may be performed by the Department as soon as possible after you receive the Certificate of Authority and have capitalized the captive. The cost of this exam will be borne by the applicant.

Steps to form a captive in New York

New York provides the following guidance from its Website:

"The following are the steps to be followed to license a captive insurer in New York:

Arrange a preliminary meeting with the New York Insurance Department's Captive Group to discuss the proposed captive and to review the licensing and incorporation process.

Obtain approval for use of the name of the captive.

Prepare and submit four completed Captive Insurance Company License Application forms (PDF Format), with all required attachments, to the NYID Captive Group including:

- A copy of the charter and bylaws or other similar documents,

- A financial statement certified by two officers and a plan of operation

- Incorporation and Licensing of the captive occurs with the direct assistance of the NYID Captive Group.

- Upon a determination that the applicant has complied with the provisions of Article 70 of the Insurance Law, a License shall be issued to the captive insurer.

General requirements:

The submitted application should include the following:
- Completed biographical for each officer and/or director

- Plan of operation

- Pro forma financials for the next five years

- Proposed charter and by-laws

- Actuarial analysis

- Loan agreement

- An independent valuation of a subsidiary may also be required

- Plan of Operation

- The plan of operation submitted with the License Application must include an actuarial report or feasibility study prepared by a qualified independent actuary. The content for the plan of operation is set forth in the Application Form. Any proposed changes to the plan of operation subsequent to licensing shall be submitted to the Superintendent thirty days before becoming effective.

Incorporation

After review of the proposed charter and by-laws by the New

York Insurance Department, the applicant will submit an executed copy of the charter. For stock insurers, an incorporation tax of one-twentieth of one percent of the par value of capital stock must be submitted to the New York Insurance Department (New York Tax Law — Section 180) at this time. The executed copy of the charter will be forwarded by the Insurance Department to the New York State Attorney General for recording and the Insurance Department will issue a Certificate of Incorporation to the captive company. After the company has been incorporated it must submit a copy of its by-laws, which shall be certified by the corporate secretary or assistant corporate secretary.

Biographical affidavit
The License Application requires submission of biographical affidavits for directors and executive officers of the proposed captive insurer. Copies should be made, completed, executed and submitted with the Application. Each Biographical Affidavit (PDF Format) form should be filled out entirely.

After incorporation, the applicant must submit:
- A certified notarized copy of the by-laws
- Appointment of Superintendent of Insurance as attorney
- Certificate of designation by captive insurer
- Board of Directors resolutions for the appointment and designation
- Proof of funding
- Appointment of Superintendent as Agent for Service of Process
- The captive insurance company shall submit a Power of Attorney (PDF Format) designating the Superintendent as agent for service of process. This shall be accompanied by a Certificate of Designation (PDF Format) naming the person to whom the Superintendent can forward any process served upon him. A certified copy of a Resolu-

tion of the Board of Directors (PDF Format) authorizing both the appointment and the designation is also required.

Other requirements to note:
Principal Office and Records
All of the books and records of the captive insurance company must be maintained at the insurer's principal office, which shall be located in New York. Books and records consist of all information and files necessary to perform an audit or examination of the captive insurer.

Board of directors
Three directors are required. The Board of Directors must hold at least one meeting in New York each year. In addition, two members of the Board must be residents of New York.

Manager
The manager of a captive insurance company shall be a person or firm resident in New York and shall be either: (1) licensed as an agent or broker in New York; or (2) approved by the Superintendent to act as a captive manager.

Post-licensing reporting requirements:
All captive insurance companies must file the New York Captive Financial Statement (PDF Format) with the NYID Captive Group by March 1st. An independent certified public accountant must opine on the financial condition of the captive insurance company on an annual basis. Loss reserves and loss expense reserves must be reported in the annual statement.

Tax and assessment filings
Tax filings and payments are made to the New York State Tax Department in accordance with the provisions of Article 33 of the New York Tax Law. Captive insurers are subject to a premium tax (referred to as a "franchise tax" under NY Tax Law) as set forth in Section 1502-b of the Tax Law. Unless capital is increased, licensed captive insurers are not taxed under any

other provision of the New York Tax Law.

Captive insurance companies must also pay an assessment pursuant to Section 332 of the New York Insurance Law, which is used to defray the operating expenses of the New York Insurance Department. The assessment is based upon the direct premiums written in New York only; non-New York and reinsurance premiums are not used in calculating the assessment. The estimated rate based upon the latest assessment available is .25% of New York direct premiums written. A Report of Premiums is filed on an annual basis with the New York Insurance Department.

Financial examination
Each captive shall be subject to an examination at least once every five years."[xvii]

Naming the captive

At some point along the way, a prospective captive owner will realize that the new captive insurance company will require a name. Assigning a name is a bit more administrative than may be the case for an organization that intends to brand its name and market its goods and services under that brand. Essentially, the name of the captive must meet the domicile requirements for naming an insurer in that jurisdiction. First the name must be unique (at least to that jurisdiction) and will likely require some standard corporate requirement such as including "incorporated," "inc." "corporation," "company" or "limited." Some domiciles may also require the name to include language indicating that the captive is in fact an insurer ("insurance," "indemnity" etc.).

Your risk management advisor or a competent corporate attorney in the domicile can help search the domicile's corporate records and file appropriate name-reservation applications to identify and reserve an available name for your captive.

Designating a registered agent for service of process

Most, if not all, domiciles will require you to name an agent for the purpose of receiving service of process. In the event that the captive is named in a lawsuit, some agent must be available to receive the service of such lawsuit. This becomes particularly important given the likelihood that the parent and captive investors will not be located in the captive's domicile. Captive domiciles want to make sure that all matters—especially ones as potentially sensitive as legal ones—will be appropriately and timely handled by every captive insurer within their jurisdictions.

Typically, the law firm identified as the captive's legal advisor for purposes of formation will serve as the captive's registered agent. Some captives will name the firm that is managing the captive in the domicile as registered agent. This is an important step in the formation process that simply can't be overlooked.

Experts and domicile-specific service providers

As should be clear from our discussion, the formation process is detailed but certainly manageable. It is during this process that companies interested in captive formation experience the full benefit of working with competent risk management advisors with specific captive formation experience. It is advisable to identify an advisor who has no specific interest in any one domicile to assist with the feasibility study, business plan development and domicile selection. Then, once a target domicile is identified, it is important to identify specific expert service providers within that domicile to assist in understanding and fully complying with the domicile's formation requirements.

At the beginning of our discussion in this chapter, we indicated that the feasibility study comes prior to completing the business plan. There may be occasions when a company is convinced that a captive formation is appropriate before conducting a feasibility study and queries whether performing that step and the associated expense is worth it. We'll address this question and the specific elements of the feasibility study in the next chapter.

Chapter 9: Is a feasibility study necessary?

At several places in this book I've addressed the need for conducting a captive feasibility study ("CFS"). In its most basic form, a CFS answers two key questions: "Is a captive insurance company right for our business?" and "If yes, what's the right organizational structure?"

As you consider forming a captive, there are many issues that must be addressed before you, and your advisors can be fully prepared to recommend a captive formation to the board of directors. The CFS is structured to perform this function. Before we discuss the specific elements of a CFS, let's address some of the most frequently asked questions about this tool.

Common questions about the captive feasibility study

1. Is a feasibility study the same as an actuarial report?
Although the actuarial report makes up a portion of the CFS, it is not the entire CFS. The actuarial report is prepared by the actuary to set an expectation of the potential losses an owner could expect in running the captive. The actuarial study may be the most important part of the feasibility study as far as determining the risks the captive should take, limits, and design

of the policies, In addition to the actuarial report, the economic and organizational components of the captive are studied in the feasibility study.

2. What are the main purposes of a feasibility study?
The CFS-process helps companies clarify their risk-financing needs and expectations. It answers the question, "What will be my return on an investment in a captive?" A quality study identifies the potential advantages and the potential risks of running a captive and insures that a company considering forming a captive is financially ready to do so.

Above and beyond the financial aspects, the feasibility study will address the specific concerns of the business. The business owner may be concerned with the business aspects of paying claims, when to deny claims, and quite often, how do they maintain business relationships with customers who feel they have a legitimate claim against the client. They may find it helpful from a business perspective to be able to pay claims to maintain future business relationships.

3. Who conducts the feasibility study?
The CFS can be conducted by a company's internal risk management, accounting, finance and legal staff; it can be conducted by a commercial insurance broker who has expertise in the captive insurance industry; it can be conducted by an independent risk-management advisor experienced in developing captive feasibility studies. Typically, all but the very largest organizations will turn to outside expertise given the specialized nature of the captive insurance industry. But in most all cases, a combination of internal and external resources produce the best product. The internal risk management, financial and legal staff are in the best position to fully communicate the company's current risk profile and the external experts are in the best position to understand the captive markets, the effectiveness of various uses and structures of captives and the differences among the various domiciles.

4. What does a feasibility study cost?

If the CFS is conducted using external resources, the risk management advisor fee will typically range from $15,000 to $25,000 depending on the complexity of the organization and its goals. Additional fees often include those for legal, tax, and actuarial analysis.

5. Is a feasibility study required for getting licensed as an insurance company?

Most U.S. domiciles expect to see (or require) a feasibility study. This requirement is not as prevalent with offshore domiciles. Generally speaking, the insurance officials want to be sure that at least some level of due diligence has taken place before applying for an insurance license and a quality CFS is a good indicator

6. How long does it take to complete a feasibility study?

Depending on the complexity of the organization's business and goals and also depending on the ready availability of loss data, it usually takes between 4 and 12 weeks to complete a feasibility study for a single-parent captive. The initial draft report is often completed in the first 2 to 8 weeks. The drafter will then allow 2 to 4 weeks for all parties to review draft and make appropriate modifications. If there are more investors involved, for example in the case of a group captive, the CFS will almost certainly take longer given the added complexities of multiple parties, multiple loss histories and possibly differing goals.

7. Should I be concerned about confidentiality?

Sometimes, potential captive owners are reluctant to complete a feasibility study as a part of the license-application process because they are not sure who has access to the application information and they naturally want to protect their confidential financial and risk-profile information. Most domiciles recognize this concern and will often address it specifically by ensuring applicants that their information will not be made public. If this is not clear in the domicile regulations, it should be addressed early on in the process so that there are no surprises down the road.

Elements of the feasibility study

Remember that a major difference between a captive insurance strategy and other insurance strategies is the capital investment. Unlike in a commercial insurance situation or a self-insured situation, a company that operates a captive must contribute capital (or at least it must tie up collateral to support a letter of credit). That is, when insurance is purchased from a commercial carrier or a company self-insures its risk, there is no requirement to put capital at risk. In the case of the former, premiums are paid to the insurer and become an expense; in the case of the latter, losses are paid as incurred—again, an expense. Any investor who puts capital at risk will want to make sure that capital is put to good use to benefit the business. Understanding *how* this investment will be utilized is where the CFS begins.

1. Clarifying the objectives

First, the CFS will make clear the objectives for the use of a captive should it ultimately be determined one is appropriate. The objectives section sets the focus of the study. Because a CFS could easily analyze thousands of issues, risks and structures, some parameters must be established. This is why feasibility studies can't be "off the shelf" boilerplate projects; they must be customized for each organization.

Despite the need for customization, some objectives will be consistent among different organizations. Most companies will undertake a feasibility study to better understand what a captive *can* do for them. As captive's are often new to the evaluating investor, this education element is very important. Most companies will also want the feasibility study to provide them with arguments either for or against forming a captive to be used for the board of directors or other decision makers. And in those domiciles where it is required, a CFS satisfies a statutory requirement as well.

> ## Captive Insight
>
> Feasibility Studies are important to the understanding of the captive owner. To see a sample of a Captive Feasibility Study, go to www.takencaptive.com and enter: "CFS" in the "**Captive Insight**" box.

2. Defining the risk

Once the objectives for conducting the CFS are clearly stated, the analysis can begin. The CFS will identify the specific risks that will be the focus of the captive. Understanding the risks that the organization is considering assigning to a captive is critical because a proper and complete risk management actuarial report can only be completed once the risks are known and clearly identified. It is not uncommon for a company to exclude certain risks from the captive based on the results of the CFS data analysis. Businesses may choose to examine risks that are currently insurable in the traditional market. They may look at what is excluded from their policies. A business often looks at the major expenses and losses that have occurred over a 10-year period to see if there is a way to craft an insurance policy to pre-fund today, a loss in the future.

Depending on the types of policies to be written and risks to be insured, the CFS will have to include an analysis on fronting and reinsurance arrangements.

A note on the actuarial study

While on the topic of defining the risk, I want to spend a moment discussion the actuarial study. This element of every due diligence process is vitally important to the success or failure of a captive. Why? Because the actuarial study is the most scientific approach to projecting claims and the cost of those claims that you will have. It typically projects the data based on loss runs for the most recent three to five years. Because actuaries use enormous amounts of industry data and very sophisticated analyses, the actuarial report that results from the study will be very valuable to you.

The actuarial data is put into the financial models to see the entire economic impact of the captive. Not only will it be a critical component of determining the feasibility of forming and operating a captive, but it will help you set rates and design the proper models for the per occurrence and aggregate stop losses. It will also provide your shareholders and the regulators with a degree of confidence in your plans. The proper actuarial study is a differentiator. If the person putting together the study does not start with the risk management side of the equation, the captive may not be formed for the proper reason.

3. Measuring the risk

Once the objectives of the study are defined and the potential risks to be included in the analysis are identified, the data analysis can begin. The data and financial analysis is the heart of the feasibility study. In the end, this analysis (that includes a competent actuarial study) will likely play the biggest role in determining whether a captive is going to be an appropriate alternative risk financing solution. Just keep in mind that it is not the only factor in this decision. A good feasibility study will evaluate the myriad of issues that go beyond the pure financial considerations to get the best picture of whether a captive is an appropriate investment.
In terms of measuring the pure financial considerations, following are some of the key components:

Retained risk and loss projections - The feasibility study will identify which risks the captive is willing to retain and at what levels. For those risks, the analysis will identify loss projections based on expected frequency and severity of claims. This data can come from the organization's historical loss experience, loss data from the commercial-insurance industry or even educated estimates if that is all that is available (e.g., for exposures that may be unique and for which there is no market data). In addition to this being valuable for determining capitalization, it is also important information for defining policy limits, premium levels and reinsurance levels.

Expense budget for the captive – The captive insurance company is and must be run like a separate, self-sustaining business. Therefore, it must have a clearly defined operating structure with associated expense budget. The CFS provides the owner the opportunity to fully understand and define this expense structure.

Tax impact - As pointed out previously, tax implications should never be the sole or even predominant reason for forming and running a captive insurance company. In fact, if there is no other compelling reason to form a captive beyond some tax advantage, you can expect the IRS to challenge the captive's existence. However, there is nothing wrong with an organization forming in such a way as to produce a favorable tax outcome.

For example, an organization may decide to form in a particular domicile because it has a lower-cost tax structure than others. That's a perfectly legitimate strategy even though it clearly reduces the amount of tax revenue the government will receive. When it comes to the financial analysis section of the CFS, a discussion of tax impact is an important component. In fact, some—if not most—domiciles expect to see this analysis. The taxes that should be addressed include:

- U.S. (or other country) income tax
- Excise taxes
- Excess and surplus lines taxes

- Domicile premiums taxes
- Local premium taxes
- Other taxes/assessments

Premium strategy – The captive will need to ensure that it has a clearly established premium rate structure and individual rates for each line of coverage. By presenting these premiums by line-of-coverage, the captive owner will be able to estimate the total expected premium contribution, which will help determine the overall required capital necessary to support the captive.

Capitalization – The reason there is a capital requirement is to ensure that the captive can support the risk that it is assuming. It makes sense for the captive to be adequately funded but not over-funded. Ultimately, capital requirements will be determined by a combination of captive-funding needs and the domicile's statutory requirements. The quality of the capital estimate will be based on the quality of the information used to arrive at those estimates. That includes the credibility of loss projections, the quality of the rate-setting process, and the claim-management procedures that will be put in place among other processes.

Pro forma financial statements – Since the captive will be an independent operating insurance concern, it will need to show profit and loss projections. A five-year horizon for the pro forma financials is appropriate. These financials should include:

- Income statements and balance sheets
- Five-year pro forma results
- Presentation of tax consequences
- Financial assumptions (interest rates, growth rates, cost of capital, etc.)

Some domiciles will provide specific guidance as to what they would like to see as a part of the financial presentation. For example, Utah's "minimum requirements" guidelines indicate:

"Pro forma financial models should include the following items:

- An income statement and balance sheet
- Parameters which agree with the other analyses in the [feasibility study]
- Include at least five years of pro forma results
- Account for the effects of all types of taxation (or explain why there are no tax consequences)
- Include at least one scenario worse than expected which demonstrates the consideration of possible financial impairment
- Include a detailed explanation of each modeling assumption
- Include general assumptions such as interest rates, year-to-year growth rates, etc.
- Include a model showing the minimum number of participants, premiums, or capital"[xviii]

It's always a good idea to look for and understand any guidance provided by those domiciles that are on the "potentials" list for your captive. It's usually much easier to address the issues during the analysis process than discovering requirements that must be worked into the CFS later.

4. Structuring strategy
The structuring section of the feasibility study will address the various captive-program structure options available to the captive owner. Based on the data analysis completed as a part of the CFS, this section will identify costs and benefits of the most likely program structures, including the need

for fronting arrangements and reinsurance. Here, the preparer of the CFS will evaluate the cash flow projections of operating the captive as a direct program versus operating the captive through another insurer—i.e., in a fronted relationship. In a fronting arrangement, the captive pays fronting fees and puts up collateral in support of a letter of credit to a traditional commercial insurer who will provide policies. This allows a captive to write any insurance that the fronting company is willing to write.

With a direct writing captive, policies are issued directly to the insured by the captive. There are no fronting fees of course, but the captive obviously must go through the licensure process. Also, because the captive will be a new insurance company, it will not have a financial rating which could be important in some circumstances. For example, some contracts require insurance from a rated insurance company (e.g., a contract provision might read: "Coverage must be with an insurance carrier having an AM Best Rating of A- or better.") A new captive will not be able to satisfy that requirement.

The CFS preparer will also evaluate the types of risks the proposed captive is considering covering as a part of the analysis to determine the most appropriate structure options.

5. Domicile choice

The CFS will identify the potential domiciles for the captive, weighing the relative advantages and disadvantages of each and the key factors that drive the domicile recommendations. We discussed choosing a domicile in chapter 4, including an overview of onshore versus offshore domiciles. The feasibility study should incorporate that analysis since the captive-program structuring decisions, financial considerations and tax consequences will significantly impact the feasibility of forming and operating a captive. The CFS will make recommendations as to the most appropriate domicile for the given assumptions.

6. Operating the captive

This portion of the CFS sets forth a plan for implementing the captive strategy. Although the details of the plan will be shaped by the captive-program structure and, to some degree, by the domicile ultimately selected, standard operating components will almost always be included. These components include identification of the captive manager, lines of business, coverages, policy forms, limits, deductibles and retentions. Also included is a review of the source of operating funds such as premium amounts, letters of credit and projected investment income.

Choosing the right partners

As this discussion about developing the captive feasibility study makes clear, every company that considers forming a captive will need the support of at least a few external service providers. As has been pointed out throughout this book, a captive must be formed and operated as a legitimate insurance company. That process typically falls outside the scope of a company's expertise given the fact that it is not the company's core business. For a potential captive owner to successfully establish and operate a captive insurance company for the long term, the right team must be in place. The challenge lies in determining just how to do that.

Over the 15 years that I have been providing risk-management and captive-insurance formation guidance, I have seen many approaches. Without hesitation, the most successful approach is the one that involves creating a team of experts who bring successful track records and who are committed to taking every step of the process seriously. Those who take short cuts or who rely on one consultant or promoter to do it all are frequently unsuccessful in operating a captive or end up with a result that does not meet the captive owner's needs. Expensive mistakes can be avoided by spending a bit of time up front to build the right team for your organization.

Building the right team: A three-step approach

1. Evaluate and select the risk-management advisor.
First, hire a risk-management advisor with a strong reputation in the captive insurance market and who has extensive experience helping companies in multiple industries develop captive insurance programs that are successful over the long-term.

When choosing an advisor in the alternative risk marketplace, it is vital to use an advisor with a firm and deep understanding of insurance and the role of risk transfer. Many of the advisors we see are not licensed in Property/Casualty insurance and therefore have limited experience in the very risk they are helping to insure. There are many places to start and a good place to find credible advisors is through the ICCIE (International Center for Captive Insurance Education).

As ICCIE was being organized, feedback from industry experts made it clear that a captive insurance education designation should be available through a comprehensive program of study. It was with this in mind that the Associate in Captive Insurance (ACI) designation program was created, and it was intentionally designed to be "challenging and complete – to assure professionals that the designation would be meaningful."[xix]
The key is for you to ask for specific examples of success and then to contact a few of the companies the consultant has assisted. It's also important to be alert to any underlying motives of a consultant. Frequently, a consultant will have a vested interest in directing business to a particular domicile or the consultant will have a particular product or products that he or she is pushing. Understanding if the consultant has experience with more than just one or two domiciles will be valuable. It would also be helpful to see some examples of recent captive structures the consultant has helped develop. If they all look the same even though

the businesses and industries are different, ask lots of questions. Some consultants get so comfortable with one domicile or one product or structure that they won't consider alternatives—alternatives that may be a better fit for your business.

2. **Evaluate and retain specialty service providers.**
   One important service the consultant will provide once retained is helping you assemble the other key players on the team. As has been discussed, these players will include professionals to handle audit, legal, actuarial and tax issues and analysis. These professionals should also be unbiased and well experienced in the captive industry. Once the captive is formed, you'll need additional professional support such as a captive manager, law firm and banking relationship located within the captive domicile. For all service providers, the consultant should have more than one recommendation for each service and be able to provide objective comments about the strengths of each.

3. **Evaluate the consultant's system for measuring performance.**
   Make sure the consultant has a system for measuring performance, for keeping the process on track and providing you solid feedback. Ask the consultant how these steps will be handled through the feasibility study process and the formation and operation process.
   By ensuring you have a competent, professional, risk-management advisor in place to quarterback the feasibility study process, to help retain the right professionals to round out the team and to ensure a successful captive-formation and operation process (should that be the determination), you are giving yourself the best chance at successfully meeting your risk-financing objectives.

Chapter 10: What's involved in managing a captive?

Once a captive insurance company is formed and licensed, the captive owner must now turn its attention to actually running the captive. Although stated several times before, it bears repeating here: a captive is an insurance company and it must be operated as such. As daunting as that may sound initially, you either have heard or will hear from captive industry consultants that managing a captive is not terribly challenging provided you have the right support team in place. While I believe that is essentially true, I also believe you should clearly understand all the requirements before you turn over the management responsibility to anyone. I believe it is a big mistake to outsource something simply because you do not understand it. You should first understand each component's role in the captive operation well enough to ask the right questions; then secure a resource expert in managing that function.

So the first step in the process is to learn the responsibilities of each captive-management function. In order to delegate the responsibilities you must know what they are. Second, no matter what partners are retained to provide management support, *you* are still ultimately responsible for the regulatory compliance of the captive. So, to repeat, it is very important for you to spend the time it takes to clearly understand the regulatory and fiduciary requirements of managing the captive.

While this chapter is no way exhaustive, it will at least give you a start—a framework to facilitate the process of understanding the key elements of effectively managing a captive insurance company.

Key components of captive management

At its highest level, captive management focuses on four key areas:

Underwriting

Claim management

Financial management

Compliance/reporting

There are certainly more functions of a captive (e.g., strategic planning, risk management, marketing and communication, etc.), but these four are important to understand up front. Each one of these areas requires specific expertise and industry knowledge. Understanding the basics will help you find the right partner for your organization.

Underwriting
Certainly you are familiar with underwriting. It is the process of reviewing and evaluating risk for potential coverage, setting premium rates, reviewing coverage applications and writing policies. The initial critical step of the underwriting process is defining the insured. In a single-parent captive, this will be one of the parent's subsidiaries (this is often referred to as "related risk"). In a group captive, it will be one member of the group. Once the insured is identified the underwriting process turns to understanding what risks are being considered. By under-

standing the risk and exposure to be underwritten, the underwriter can determine whether the risk is appropriate for the captive to cover and if so, how much of the risk to cover and what that coverage should cost.

Captive Insight

Did you know that the term "underwriting" came from the insurance market in London? When a ship was to set sail, those investors who agreed to accept some of the risk of the loss of that ship in exchange for a premium would write their names under the voyage information contained on a document prepared by Lloyd's of London—thereby *underwriting* the risk of loss.

The underwriting process also requires the establishment of underwriting policy. Before the first policy is written, there should be established guidelines that the underwriter should follow. This policy guidance ranges from establishing the timeline for coverage review to the required financial strength of the insured. Underwriting policy should also cover how policy terminations or loss of coverage is handled. It should also cover any target market or geographic restrictions.

A clear underwriting policy is necessary to ensure that the captive is indeed operating as an insurance company. But it is also important because the captive will likely be approaching the reinsurance market for excess and other types of coverage. The reinsurance market expects to see a legitimate operation in place and expects to see an underwriting process in place that demonstrates appropriate evaluation of the risk covered. Part of this process, and part of the reinsurers' evaluation will surround the quality of the underwriting team. They will want to know that the risk evaluation supporting the policies written (against which they are evaluating whether or not to supply supplemental coverage) is conducted by qualified professionals.

Some captives may have enough volume that they can justify having a fulltime underwriter, or a fulltime team of underwriters. Many captives however, choose to outsource this function to an organization that is in the business of providing underwriting services. Even if the captive board decides to allow staff members of the parent (such as qualified risk management professionals) to perform some of the underwriting tasks, they may not have them perform all such tasks. In fact, there are certain functions that should be performed by completely external parties who can function in an "arm's length" capacity.

One key question with underwriting will be how much authority will be vested with the underwriter? The captive board must decide how much authority it will delegate and how much it will retain when making underwriting decisions.

Every captive has different needs and different challenges. A competent risk management advisor can provide more detail around how to effectively structure the underwriting process based on the needs of your particular captive.

Claims management
Deciding what risk to underwrite is an important first step of the captive operations process. Equally important is having a mechanism in place to handle the claims that result from the policies written. In fact, this step should be carefully considered before any risk is underwritten given that the claim management system must be capable of handling the volume and type of claim that could result from the underwritten risk.

The claims management structure and the resources needed to support it will vary significantly depending on the size of the captive, the type of risk underwritten and the captive board's philosophy on managing claims. For example, some boards may decide that all claims management functions should be outsourced. Others may decide to build a claims management department or, in the case of a single-parent captive, utilize the parent's claims management operations for either a portion or all of the claims investigation and settlement process. In either case (utilizing an internal claims management group or retaining an outsourced third party), the captive board will retain ultimate settlement authority. The extent of any delegated authority—for example for the settlement of the smallest or most routine claims—must be carefully detailed in a published claims management policy developed for the captive.

As a practice, detailing the claims management policies and procedures is just good business. What's more, the captive's board will require it, some captive domiciles will expect it and some reinsurers may make it a condition of providing reinsurance coverage.

Other claims management matters to consider include defining roles, responsibilities and authority levels for all those involved in the process; establishing case-reserve protocol; and identifying and retaining the law firm that will handle litigation or other negotiations requiring legal expertise.

Clearly defining the claims management policies and procedures will become part of the captive's business planning. A competent risk management advisor with experience working in the captive industry can be very helpful to the captive owner navigating this process. The advisor will have been down this road many times before and will be able to address common scenarios and provide insight into specific domicile requirements.

Financial management
While nothing about managing a captive insurance company is unimportant, it can be safely said that financial management is among the most important functions. After all, the captive *is* a

financial management tool. Management of this function will likely involve more of the captive owner's internal resources than any other operations management function. This is not to say that there will be fewer external resources involved, however. The captive will influence risk financing decisions, tax decisions, capitalization decisions, cash management decisions, capital investment decisions, and so on. So, while there will need to be professionals with specific captive financial management expertise involved, the captive owner's chief financial officer, controller, treasurer, and tax specialist will all take an ongoing role in assisting with the financial management and financial planning around the use of the captive. This is true regardless of whether the captive is a single-parent captive or a group captive.

Sound captive financial management starts with a clear understanding of the captive insurance company's objectives—its core purpose(s) for existence. For some, this objective is to improve risk management efforts through a more customized and targeted strategy than is available in the traditional insurance market. For others, the primary objective of the captive is to build and maintain wealth through innovative risk financing and tax management strategies. Still others will operate the captive to stabilize the company's earnings or transfer wealth through more efficient risk, financial and tax management mechanisms. Whatever objectives are driving your decision to form and operate a captive insurance company, they should be clearly articulated in your captive business plan and revisited often to ensure the operation of the captive is consistent with those goals.

With the objectives for forming the captive in mind, the captive owner should develop the board policies related to the captive's financial management. Board policies establish the foundation for managing the financial functions of the captive. Once the board decides what functions will be managed internally, what will be outsourced and what level of board oversight is required, the policies can be drafted.

Typical board policies address signature/wire transfer authority, cash management and other accounting policies, risk limitation and operating ratios, investment policy, internal and external compliance communications, and contract signature authority.

Once the standard board policies and procedures based on the objectives and special needs of the captive are established, the day-to-day captive financial management can begin. Much of the financial management function is managed with routine monthly, quarterly and annual reporting. While the board members may have decided to outsource much or most of the financial management of the captive, they will stay closely connected to the performance of the captive through careful analysis of this routine internal performance reporting (to be distinguished from external, regulatory compliance reporting).

Although the routine financial reports—income statement, balance sheet, statements of cash flows, etc.—will appear familiar on the surface to most board members, it won't take long for the financial analysis to begin looking very different. Captives are insurance companies and the insurance industry is just different from what many professionals who operate outside the industry are accustomed to seeing. Because of these differences, it is important for the captive owner to help adequately prepare non-industry board members with some basic education. In addition, the board members should understand how to use helpful financial analysis tools favored in the industry.

As an example, one of the most valuable tools in terms of evaluating the financial health of the captive is the measure of capital and surplus. In fact, many believe that this is the most important metric as it provides a quick view of whether the assets positioned to support the captives' liabilities are adequate given the risk and confidence levels.

Other important metrics include the adequacy of loss reserves. The captive manager will develop reserve estimates using historical claim rates, current claim volume and anticipated future claims. Reserves will be sensitive to the types of claims written (e.g., whether they are long- or short-tail claims) and the predictability of claim frequency and severity. These loss reserves should be measured against regular actuarial estimates and should fall within a tight range of those estimates (e.g., 4-6%). With sound reserve estimates and adequate levels of capital and surplus, the captive's board can effectively use key ratios to further evaluate the financial health of the captive.

These ratios can be categorized as operating ratios and financial leverage ratios. Operating ratios, which include loss expense ratio, return on revenue ratio and investment ratio provide insight into the relationship between underwriting expense and income generated from premiums and investments.

Compliance/reporting
Any captive owner that is a publicly traded company or has some exposure to the far-reaching arms of the Sarbanes Oxley Act of 2002 will anticipate that operating an insurance company will have compliance and reporting implications. There is certainly no question that this is true. However, the reporting and compliance issues for a captive insurance company are not as onerous as those for a traditional insurance company. This is because the captive insurance companies are not offering insurance to the public. Those who are buying insurance coverage through a captive are assumed to be sophisticated buyers and so, for public-policy reasons, there are not as many compliance and reporting gates to navigate. This does not mean that this process can be taken lightly. The captive owner must be intimately aware of the various reporting requirements and must be diligent in ensuring all compliance matters are handled adequately and timely.

Each domicile has specific reporting requirements. The domicile's captive regulations will identify the type of reports it requires and the frequency of those filings. You will find that these filings and their frequency are similar among the domiciles—certainly among the domestic domiciles. As an example, consider Vermont's requirements:

"An association captive insurance company doing business in this state shall annually submit to the commissioner a report of its financial condition, verified by oath of two of its executive officers. . . .

All companies shall have an annual audit by an independent certified public accountant, authorized by the commissioner and shall file such audited financial report with the commissioner on or before   June 30 for the year ending December 31 immediately preceding. The annual audit report shall be considered part of the company's annual report of financial condition except with respect to the date by which it must be filed with the commissioner. The annual audit shall consist of the following:

A) Opinion of Independent Certified Public Accountant ...

B) Report of Evaluation of Internal Controls ...

C) Accountant's Letter ...

D) Financial Statements ...

E) Certification of Loss Reserves and Loss Expense Reserves ..."[xx]

In addition to the routine filings required by the insurance department, other regulatory agencies within the domicile will likely have their own filing requirements. All filing requirements will become part of the captive operating procedures and incorporated into an operating procedures manual the captive manager will use to ensure filing compliance.

In addition to the reporting requirements, captives have compliance responsibilities that may or may not relate directly to just the timely filing of reports. For example, many domiciles require captives to agree to an organizational review at the request of the insurance department. The goal is to ensure that appropriate operational procedures are in place and the captive is prepared to handle the functions its business plan anticipates. In addition, domiciles may require captives to submit for approval the names of auditors and actuaries the captive selects to perform financial functions. They also frequently require captives to submit to the department of insurance the names and backgrounds of all officers and directors of the captive. In fact, many domiciles will only allow a captive to use outsourced professionals that are formally approved by the department of insurance to perform the function for which they have qualified. This is the domicile's way of developing some level of predictability of operational scrutiny and operational success.

It should go without saying that managing the captive domicile's compliance and reporting requirements is of the highest importance. An experienced risk management advisor can help the new captive understand the requirements and construct the appropriate checklists and operating procedures that will keep the captive out of trouble.

Effectively managing a captive is about understanding the core requirements of operating an insurance company for the owner's articulated purposes, making sure appropriate professionals are in place to perform the relevant functions, complying with the regulatory requirements and timely reporting results. You can learn more about the details of this process at www.TakenCaptive.com.

Chapter 11: Advanced concepts

Up to this point, we've focused on understanding the basics of captive insurance companies. We've introduced how they work, how to organize them and some practical applications. But beyond the basic, traditional uses for captives, there are some very useful applications of this flexible, financial planning instrument.

For example, in certain circumstances, a captive can be used in ways that provide powerful estate-planning benefits. In such situations, we'll determine a potential captive owner's overall estate value, current estate plan, number of children, structure of any irrevocable trusts, and so on. With this information, we can craft a captive to accomplish many estate-planning goals while serving legitimate insurance purposes. In many of my lectures on captive insurance companies, I use the concept of "double duty dollars." If the captive owner has a large estate, he cannot get enough money out of the estate to make a substantial difference.

Because of the significant potential estate-planning benefits presented by captives, those evaluating the use of a captive are advised to secure advice from insurance managers who are very familiar with estate and asset protection planning.

Very few (if any) business owners that set up captives do not have a potential estate-tax problem. A common potential problem for a business owner is captive ownership. Oftentimes, a captive is owned by a business owner who has children. Many times the captive is actually owned by a separate entity owned by the children and controlled by the business owner. With this type of arrangement the business owner would potentially realize substantial benefits. With this design it is important for the business owner to set up the captive so the children do not have direct ownership. If they do, their potential creditors (and business partners, ex-spouses, etc.) could have access to the huge pile of money that will be created in a captive.

We often consider structuring the captive so it is owned by a limited partnership or an LLC (or their counterparts the Family Limited Partnership or Family Limited Liability Company). The captive owner may be able to realize substantial estate and income tax benefits by structuring the plan as follows:

In Figure 11.1 (below), the captive is owned by a Delaware limited partnership. The general partner is the business owner or (preferably) another corporation and 98% is owned by an irrevocable trust for the adult children.

Figure 11.1 – Typical captive ownership for estate planning

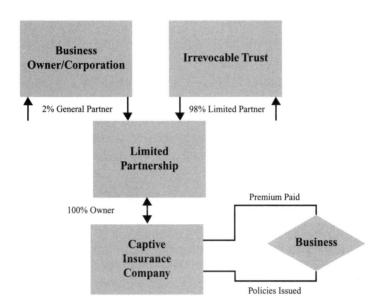

There are many estate planning benefits from this type of trust structure. Under this type of arrangement, the business owner permanently and irrevocable transfers assets to the trust. Although the business own does not keep any interest in the trust, the use of an irrevocable trust gives the business owner more control than giving the children an outright gift.

Many of the benefits involve the value of the estate and protection against the children (and their creditor). Using this trust arrangement the assets that go to the children will be outside the estate of the business owner, and the value will be greatly discounted for estate tax purposes. The patriarch (or matriarch) will transfer money to the children when the value of the insurance company is at its smallest amount, so all of the growth of the captive will not be includable in the parent's estate.

The beneficiaries of the trust are also protected in this type of arrangement. No business owner would knowingly transfer money to a child if they knew that money could be lost to the children's creditors. This arrangement will protect the heirs on three fronts. First, they have the protection of a limited partnership to protect the assets. A limited partnership has some unique features that could make it undesirable for a creditor attack. Second, the assets are inside a trust that has been designed to minimize access to the assets by the children and their creditors. We often use these trusts to protect the beneficiaries from divorce or lawsuits they may have in their own lives or businesses. Lastly, you have the protection of the insurance regulator in your domicile. No regulator is going to take assets out of the reserves of a captive to pay a non-involved judgment creditor. The regulator's job is to protect the assets of the captive to pay potential claims.

From this structure discussion, we then consider asset protection planning elements. This is almost always relevant given that nearly all of our clients have significant asset- protection concerns.

In my book on asset protection titled, "You Can Make It, But Can You Keep It?" I discuss a myriad of asset protection issues and strategies. Here is an excerpt:

"financial advisors and how-to books universally give asset protection the short shrift, focusing instead on asset building. Many investors, and even advisors, consider risk management and asset protection a shady business, speciously equating legal and appropriate wealth protection strategies with skirting their responsibilities. They carry around the preconceived notion that protecting assets is somehow immoral or unethical, and any discussion about wealth protection and risk management is condemned or condoned.

But let us consider today's environment. The slim cadre of

the ultra rich businessmen and women pay the most in taxes, even though they likely use the least amount of public services: They send their children to private schools, pay for their own health care and, when necessary, hire their own attorneys. They create jobs, and then turn around to find themselves the victims of lawsuits initiated by their clients and employees. And their fates are not determined by juries of their peers; rather, they face a class warfare system whereby the *have nots* are eager to take from the *haves*, as evidenced by the increase in runaway jury verdicts. The ultra rich use their money productively—investing it, growing it, and bolstering the economy—but even the politicians who benefit from their efforts vilify these wealthy creators. Instead of attempting to raise the poor to middle class status, government policies focus on taxing and fining the rich and prosperous simply for having the audacity to be successful."

As you can tell from the tone of the book and the focus of my practice, I am a firm believer in the value of risk management. Wealth protection may not be at the forefront of all of our client's minds, but risk management is. They may be interested in minimizing the risk of estate taxes, income taxes, improper insurance, poor business structures, or asset protection. Most often it is a combination of many of these.

Another captive-insurance structure that has value for those with asset protection concerns is similar to the example we just provided; however, instead of the limited partner being an irrevocable trust for the kids, we substitute an offshore irrevocable asset protection trust. Under this structure, we keep 100% of the assets in the U.S., all of the control with the general partner and the safety of knowing a judgment creditor will have to fight the battle overseas to get to any assets. With a properly designed foreign asset protection trust, the owner has a trust protector, the ability to move the trusts to different jurisdictions and with some countries, a structure that is by law, lawsuit proof.

**Figure 11.2 – Typical captive ownership structure for asset
protection planning**

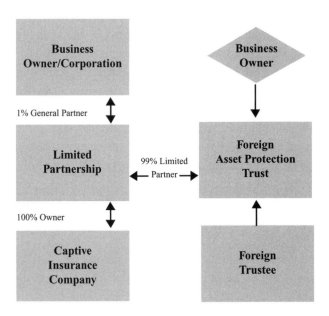

A captive structure we often explore is designed to align the
goals of a company and its employees. My background is in
structuring compensation plans for mid- to large private companies. My firm was often engaged by a client to review its
compensation plans. Most of the time, we found that the bonus
plans did not reward and encourage the desired behavior. In
other words, the employees frequently were awarded bonuses
for activity that did not drive the goals of the company. In appropriate situations, we have used captives to awards employees when their desired behavior congruent with the goals of
the business owner.

As an example, we recently formed a captive in which the key
employees have 20% ownership. In this case, the coverage written by the captive covers a risk that represents a problem area

in the business. On the one hand, since the executives of the company have an ownership stake in the captive, if there are underwriting profits, they win. On the other hand, if they cannot control the problem representing the covered risk and losses occur, they will not realize their potential financial benefit.

If this structure was not in place, the alternative executive incentive compensation plan paid cash bonuses based on overall company performance. The bonuses represented taxable income to the executives and did not foster the long- term financial goals of the employer. Owning shares of the captive creates sustained long-term positive behaviors in the executives. Taking this approach produces large financial advantages for the executives in the following way: Instead of taking ordinary income today, paying taxes on it, investing the money and paying taxes on the growth, the executives get stock in the captive, don't pay taxes today, grow the money tax deferred in the captive. The captive keeps the excess reserves and surplus shielded from the creditors of the business and the executives and upon exit the executives have the ability to take the underwriting profits as a long term capital gains not ordinary income. So in this case, the company wins because its executives are provided appropriate long-term incentive focused on key business issues and the executives benefit by gaining and keeping more long-term compensation.

In addition to the ability to retain key employees, there are some other benefits a business owner would derive from a using a captive for employees and their benefits. Many employees are not interested in the financial aspects of a captive but in the quality of the benefits they get being employed. Employee benefit captives give the business owner three main benefits: better coverage, tax efficiency and unrelated business for distribution.

An employee benefit captive will give the business owner the ability to tailor the coverage to meet the individual needs of their employees. The employer knows the workforce so they are in the best position to include benefits desired by the workers and exclude coverage that in not important to the work force, thus saving money on premiums. The employer has the ability currently to do this outside of the captive by going self insured.

As mentioned earlier, self-insurance has the problem of not being deductible when premiums are set aside. Funding these benefits into a captive may now be a deductible expense. An employee benefit captive will also help the captive justify risk distribution and unrelated business risk. According to Revenue Ruling 92-93, the IRS will treat the lives of the employees as unrelated risk for distribution testing.

Using this approach to qualify for unrelated risk has a few requirements, but significantly increases the probability the premiums paid by the parent company completely deductible. We have found there can be significant cost savings to employers that put some employee benefits into a captive insurance program. The ability to utilize a captive for these benefits will depend on the type of business, risks they face, and losses they have incurred in the past.

These were just a few examples of how a business owner could use the captive in new and exciting ways. Whether a business owner is interested in lowering the cost of insurance, designing more complete coverage, doing estate planning, or wealth protection, a captive can be a great tool to help them achieve their goals. As with most good ideas, "the devil is in the details."

Some Final Words

Captives are a complex, fascinating, wonderful financial vehicle that for the right client there will be nothing better. For the wrong client, there may be nothing worse. I hope you found this book to be a helpful resource as you explore the world of captives.

Please continue to check the website for up to the minute information on captives, IRS memos, rulings, etc. We continually update www.takencaptive.com with articles, white papers and case studies you may find useful.

Good Luck, thank you for investing your time in reading this book, and please contact us with any questions, or comments you have.

Appendix A: Vermont Irrevocable Letter of Credit

STATE OF VERMONT
CAPTIVE INSURANCE COMPANY
IRREVOCABLE LETTER OF CREDIT

Letter of Credit No. (00001)
Date

A.B.C. Bank
Address
City, State
Commissioner of Banking, Insurance, Securities and
Health Care Administration
State of Vermont
89 Main Street
Montpelier, VT 05620-3101

Commissioner:

1. We hereby establish our IRREVOCABLE LETTER OF CREDIT in your favor for the account of _____ up to the aggregate amount of _____ available by your draft(s) drawn on us, at sight, bearing the number of this IRREVOCABLE LETTER OF CREDIT No. (00001). This LETTER OF CREDIT shall expire at our Letter of Credit Department, _____, at our close of business on _____ unless as hereinafter extended.

2. This LETTER OF CREDIT is issued pursuant to the provisions of Sections 6004 of Chapter 141 of 8 Vermont Statutes Annotated, and on behalf of the above mentioned _____ (name of captive) which is applying for a certificate of authority to engage in the insurance business in the State of Vermont as a captive insurance com-

pany. We understand and agree that _____
(name of captive) has no obligation to reimburse us and we
have no right of set off against any funds held by us for
_____ (name of captive) in the event this
LETTER OF CREDIT is drawn down, in whole or in part. By
issuing this LETTER OF CREDIT, we waive any common law,
statutory or contractual right of reimbursement or set off
against_____ (name of captive) that may
arise in the event this LETTER OF CREDIT is drawn down, in
whole or in part.

3. It is a condition of the LETTER OF CREDIT that it shall be
automatically extended for additional periods, each of one year,
unless at least ninety calendar days prior to the then relevant
expiration date we have advised you in writing, by certified
mail, that we elect not to extend. In that event, you may draw
hereunder on or prior to the then relevant expiration date, up to
the full amount then available hereunder, against your sight
draft(s) on us, bearing the number of this LETTER OF
CREDIT.

4. It is a further condition of this LETTER OF CREDIT that
each automatic extension shall be measured from the then relevant expiration date, even though such date is not a business
day in Montpelier, Vermont for this Bank. It is also a condition of this LETTER OF CREDIT that, for the purpose of
drawing hereunder, if the then relevant expiration date is a non-
business day for our Bank, drawing may be made not later than
our next immediately following business day.

5. This LETTER OF CREDIT sets forth in full the terms
of our undertaking, and such undertaking shall not in any way
be modified, amended or amplified by reference to any note,
document, instrument, statute, regulation or agreement
referred to herein or in which this LETTER OF CREDIT is
referred to or to which this LETTER OF CREDIT relates and
any such reference shall not be deemed to incorporate herein
by reference any note, document, instrument, statute, regulation, or agreement.

6. Each sight draft so drawn and presented shall be promptly honored by us if presented on or prior to the above stated expiration date or any extension thereof as above provided. Presentation under this LETTER OF CREDIT must be made at _____ located at _____ during normal banking hours.

7. Unless otherwise expressly stated, this undertaking is issued subject to the International Standby Practices 1998 (ISP 98), ICC Publication No. 590.

Very truly yours,

Department of Banking, Ins., Securities & Health Care Administration 89 Main St, Montpelier, VT 05620-3101 FORM E-702 2/07

Appendix B: Relevant IRS Regulations

REVENUE RULE 2005-40

Law

Section 831(a) of the Internal Revenue Code provides that taxes, computed as provided in § 11, are imposed for each taxable year on the taxable income of each insurance company other than a life insurance company. Section 831(c) provides that, for purposes of § 831, the term "insurance company" has the meaning given to such term by § 816(a). Under § 816(a), the term "insurance company" means any company more than half of the business of which during the taxable year is the issuing of insurance or annuity contracts or the reinsuring of risks underwritten by insurance companies.

Section 162(a) provides, in part, that there shall be allowed as a deduction all the ordinary and necessary expenses paid or incurred during the taxable year in carrying on any trade or business. Section 1.162-1(a) of the Income Tax Regulations provides, in part, that among the items included in business expenses are insurance premiums against fire, storms, theft, accident, or other similar losses in the case of a business. Neither the Code nor the regulations define the terms "insurance" or "insurance contract." The United States Supreme Court, however, has explained that in order for an arrangement to constitute insurance for federal income tax purposes, both risk shifting and risk distribution must be present. Helvering v. Le Gierse, 312 U.S. 531 (1941). The risk transferred must be risk of economic loss. Allied Fidelity Corp. v. Commissioner, 572 F.2d 1190, 1193 (7th Cir.), cert. denied, 439 U.S. 835 (1978). The risk must contemplate the fortuitous occurrence of a stated contingency, Commissioner v. Treganowan, 183 F.2d 288, 290-91 (2d Cir.), cert. denied, 340 U.S. 853 (1950), and must not be merely an investment or business risk. Le Gierse, at 542; Rev. Rul. 89-96, 1989-2 C.B. 114. Risk shifting occurs if a person facing the possibility of an economic loss transfers some or all of the financial consequences of the potential loss to the insurer, such that a loss by the insured does not affect the insured because the loss is offset by a payment from the insurer. Risk distribution incorporates the statistical phenomenon known as the law of large numbers. Distributing risk allows the insurer to reduce the possibility that a single costly claim will exceed the amount taken in as premiums and set aside for the payment of such a claim. By assuming numerous relatively small, independent risks that occur randomly over time, the insurer smooths out losses to match more closely its receipt of premiums. Clougherty Packing Co. v. Commissioner, 811 F.2d 1297, 1300 (9th Cir. 1987). Courts have recognized that risk distribution necessarily entails a pooling of premiums, so that a potential insured is not in significant part paying for its own risks. Humana, Inc. v. Commissioner, 881 F.2d 247, 257 (6th Cir. 1989). See also Ocean Drilling & Exploration Co. v. United States, 988 F.2d 1135, 1153 (Fed. Cir. 1993) ("Risk distribution involves spreading the risk of loss among policyholders."); Beech Aircraft Corp. v. United States, 797 F.2d 920, 922 (10th Cir. 1986) ("'[R]isk distributing' means that the party assuming the risk distributes his potential liability, in part, among others."); Treganowan, at 291 (quoting Note, *The New York Stock Exchange Gratuity Fund:Insurance that Isn't Insurance*, 59 Yale L. J. 780, 784 (1950)) ("'By diffusing the risks through a mass of separate risk shifting contracts, the insurer casts his lot with the law of averages. The process of risk distribution, therefore, is the very essence of insurance.'"); Crawford Fitting Co. v. United States, 606 F. Supp. 136, 147 (N.D. Ohio 1985) ("[T]he court finds . . . that various nonaffiliated persons or entities facing risks similar but independent of those faced by plaintiff were named insureds under the policy, enabling the distribution of the risk thereunder."); AMERCO and Subsidiaries v. Commissioner, 96 T.C. 18, 41 (1991), aff'd, 979 F.2d 162 (9th Cir. 1992) ("The concept of risk-distributing emphasizes the pooling aspect of insurance: that it is the nature of an insurance contract to be part of a larger collection of coverages, combined to distribute risk between insureds.").

REVENUE RULE 2002-89

Internal Revenue Service (I.R.S.) Revenue Ruling

Captive insurance

Section 801.—Tax Imposed, 26 CFR 1.801-3: Definitions.

A revenue ruling that sets forth circumstances under which arrangements between a domestic parent corporation and its wholly owned insurance subsidiary constitute insurance for Federal income tax purposes.

Section 831.—Tax on Insurance Companies Other Than Life Insurance Companies, 26 CFR 1.831-3: Tax on insurance companies (other than life or mutual), mutual marine insurance companies, mutual fire insurance companies issuing perpetual policies, and mutual fire and flood insurance companies operating on the basis of premium deposits; taxable years beginning after December 31, 1962.

A revenue ruling that sets forth circumstances under which arrangements between a domestic parent corporation and its wholly owned insurance subsidiary constitute insurance for Federal income tax purposes.

Section 162.—Trade or Business Expenses, 26 CFR 1.162-1: Business expenses.

Captive insurance. This ruling considers circumstances under which arrangements between a domestic parent corporation and its wholly owned insurance subsidiary constitute insurance for federal income tax purposes. Rev. Rul. 2001-31 amplified.

Issue

Are the amounts paid by a domestic parent corporation to its wholly owned insurance subsidiary deductible as "insurance premiums" under § 162 of the Internal Revenue Code?

Facts

Situation 1. P, a domestic corporation, enters into an annual arrangement with its wholly owned domestic subsidiary S whereby S "insures" the professional liability risks of P either directly or as a reinsurer of these risks. S is regulated as an insurance company in each state where S does business.

The amounts P pays to S under the arrangement are established according to customary industry rating formulas. In all respects, the parties conduct themselves consistently with the standards applicable to an insurance arrangement between unrelated parties.

In implementing the arrangement, S may perform all necessary administrative tasks, or it may outsource those tasks at prevailing commercial market rates. P does not provide any guarantee of S's performance, and all funds and business records of P and S are separately maintained. S does not loan any funds to P.

In addition to the arrangement with P, S enters into insurance contracts whereby S serves as a direct insurer or a reinsurer of the professional liability risks of entities unrelated to P or S. The risks of unrelated entities and those of P are homogeneous. The amounts S receives from these unrelated entities under these insurance contracts likewise are established according to customary industry rating formulas.

The premiums S earns from the arrangement with P constitute 90% of S's total premiums earned during the taxable year on both a gross and net basis. The liability coverage S provides to P accounts for 90% of the total risks borne by S.

Situation 2. Situation 2 is the same as Situation 1 except that the premiums S earns from the arrangement with P constitute less than 50% of S's total premiums earned during the taxable year on both a gross and net basis. The liability coverage S provides to P accounts for less that 50% of the total risks borne by S.

Law and analysis

Section 162(a) of the Code provides, in part, that there shall be allowed as a deduction all the ordinary and necessary expenses paid or incurred during the taxable year in carrying on any trade or business.

Section 1.162-1(a) of the Income Tax Regulations provides, in part, that among the items included in business expenses are insurance premiums against fire, storms, theft, accident, or other similar losses in the case of a business.

Neither the Code nor the regulations define the terms "insurance" or "insurance contract." The United States Supreme Court, however, has explained that in order for an arrangement to constitute insurance for federal income tax purposes, both risk shifting and risk distribution must be present. Helvering v. LeGierse, 312 U.S. 531 (1941).

Risk shifting occurs if a person facing the possibility of an economic loss transfers some or all of the financial consequences of the potential loss to the insurer, such that a loss by the insured does not affect the insured because the loss is offset by the insurance payment. Risk distribution incorporates the statistical phenomenon known as the law of large numbers. Distributing risk allows the insurer to reduce the possibility that a single costly claim will exceed the amount taken in as premiums and set aside for the payment of such a claim. By assuming numerous relatively small, independent risks that occur randomly over time, the insurer smooths out losses to match more closely its receipt of premiums. Clougherty Packing Co. v. Commissioner, 811 F.2d 1297, 1300 (9th Cir. 1987). Risk distribution necessarily entails a pooling of premiums, so that a potential insured is not in significant part paying for its own risks. See Humana, Inc. v. Commissioner, 881 F.2d 247, 257 (6th Cir. 1989).

No court has held that a transaction between a parent and its wholly-owned subsidiary satisfies the requirements of risk shifting and risk distribution if only the risks of the parent are "insured." See Stearns-Roger Corp. v. United States, 774 F.2d

414 (10th Cir. 1985); Carnation Co. v. Commissioner, 640 F.2d 1010 (9th Cir. 1981), cert. denied 454 U.S. 965 (1981). However, courts have held that an arrangement between a parent and its subsidiary can constitute insurance because the parent's premiums are pooled with those of unrelated parties if (i) insurance risk is present, (ii) risk is shifted and distributed, and (iii) the transaction is of the type that is insurance in the commonly accepted sense. See, e.g., Ocean Drilling & Exploration Co. v. United States, 988 F.2d 1135 (Fed. Cir. 1993); AMERCO, Inc. v. Commissioner, 979 F.2d 162 (9th Cir. 1992).

S is regulated as an insurance company in each state in which it transacts business, and the arrangements between P and S and between S and entities unrelated to P or S are established and conducted consistently with the standards applicable to an insurance arrangement. P does not guarantee S's performance and S does not make any loans to P; P's and S's funds and records are separately maintained. The narrow question presented in Situation 1 and Situation 2 is whether S underwrites sufficient risks of unrelated parties that the arrangement between P and S constitutes insurance for federal income tax purposes.

In Situation 1, the premiums that S earns from its arrangement with P constitute 90% of its total premiums earned during the taxable year on both a gross and a net basis. The liability coverage S provides to P accounts for 90% of the total risks borne by S. No court has treated such an arrangement between a parent and its wholly-owned subsidiary as insurance. To the contrary, the arrangement lacks the requisite risk shifting and risk distribution to constitute insurance for federal income tax purposes.

In Situation 2, the premiums that S earns from its arrangement with P constitute less than 50% of the total premiums S earned during the taxable year on both a gross and a net basis. The liability coverage S provides to P accounts for less than 50% of the total risks borne by S. The premiums and risks of P are thus pooled with those of the unrelated insureds. The requisite risk shifting and risk distribution to constitute insurance for federal income tax purposes are present. The arrangement is insurance in the commonly accepted sense.

Holdings

In Situation 1, the arrangement between P and S does not constitute insurance for federal income tax purposes, and amounts paid by P to S pursuant to that arrangement are not deductible as "insurance premiums" under § 162.

In Situation 2, the arrangement between P and S constitutes insurance for federal income tax purposes, and the amounts paid by P to S pursuant to that arrangement are deductible as "insurance premiums" under § 162.

REVENUE RULE 2002-90

Internal Revenue Service (I.R.S.) Revenue Ruling

Captive insurance

Whether a transaction where amounts are paid for professional liability coverage by a number of domestic operating subsidiaries to an insurance subsidiary of a common parent constitutes insurance for Federal income tax purposes?

Captive insurance. This ruling considers circumstances under which payments for professional liability coverage by a number of operating subsidiaries to an insurance subsidiary of a common parent constitute insurance for federal income tax purposes. Rev. Rul. 2001-31 amplified.

Captive insurance. This ruling considers circumstances under which payments for professional liability coverage by a number of operating subsidiaries to an insurance subsidiary of a common parent constitute insurance for federal income tax purposes.

Issue

Are the amounts paid for professional liability coverage by domestic operating subsidiaries to an insurance subsidiary of a common parent deductible as "insurance premiums" under § 162 of the Internal Revenue Code?

Facts

P, a domestic holding company, owns all of the stock of 12 domestic subsidiaries that provide professional services. Each subsidiary in the P group has a geographic territory comprised of a state in which the subsidiary provides professional services. The subsidiaries in the P group operate on a decentralized basis. The services provided by the employees of each subsidiary are performed under the general guidance of a supervisory professional for a particular facility of the subsidiary. The general categories of the professional services rendered by each of the subsidiaries are the same throughout the P group. Together the 12 subsidiaries have a significant volume of independent, homogeneous risks.

P, for a valid non-tax business purpose, forms S as a wholly-owned insurance subsidiary under the laws of State C. P provides S adequate capital and S is fully licensed in State C and in the 11 other states where the respective operating subsidiaries conduct their professional service businesses. S directly insures the professional liability risks of the 12 operating subsidiaries in the P group. S charges the 12 subsidiaries arms-length premiums, which are established according to customary industry rating formulas. None of the operating subsidiaries have liability coverage for less than 5%, nor more than 15%, of the total risk insured by S. S retains the risks that it insures from the 12 operating subsidiaries. There are no parental (or other related party) guarantees of any kind made in favor of S. S does not loan any funds to P or to the 12 operating subsidiaries. In all respects, the parties conduct themselves in a manner consistent with the standards applicable to an insurance arrangement between unrelated parties. S does not provide coverage to any entity other than the 12 operating subsidiaries.

Law and analysis

Section 162(a) of the Code provides, in part, that there shall be allowed as a deduction all the ordinary and necessary expenses paid or incurred during the taxable year in carrying on any trade or business.

Section 1.162-1(a) of the Income Tax Regulations provides, in part, that among the items included in business expenses are insurance premiums against fire, storms, theft, accident, or other similar losses in the case of a business.

Neither the Code nor the regulations define the terms "insurance" or "insurance contract." The United States Supreme Court, however, has explained that in order for an arrangement to constitute "insurance" for federal income tax purposes, both risk shifting and risk distribution must be present. Helvering v.

LeGierse, 312 U.S. 531 (1941).

Risk shifting occurs if a person facing the possibility of an economic loss transfers some or all of the financial consequences of the potential loss to the insurer, such that a loss by the insured does not affect the insured because the loss is offset by the insurance payment. Risk distribution incorporates the statistical phenomenon known as the law of large numbers. Distributing risk allows the insurer to reduce the possibility that a single costly claim will exceed the amount taken in as premiums and set aside for the payment of such a claim. By assuming numerous relatively small, independent risks that occur randomly over time, the insurer smooths out losses to match more closely its receipt of premiums. Clougherty Packing Co. v. Commissioner, 811 F.2d 1297, 1300 (9th Cir. 1987). Risk distribution necessarily entails a pooling of premiums, so that a potential insured is not in significant part paying for its own risks. See Humana Inc. v. Commissioner, 881 F.2d 247, 257 (6th Cir. 1989).

In Humana, the United States Court of Appeals for the Sixth Circuit held that arrangements between a parent corporation and its insurance company subsidiary did not constitute insurance for federal income tax purposes. The court also held, however, that arrangements between the insurance company subsidiary and several dozen other subsidiaries of the parent (operating an even larger number of hospitals) qualified as insurance for federal income tax purposes because the requisite risk shifting and risk distribution were present. But see Malone & Hyde, Inc. v. Commissioner, 62 F.3d 835 (6th Cir. 1995) (concluding the lack of a business purpose, the undercapitalization of the offshore captive insurance subsidiary and the existence of related party guarantees established that the substance of the transaction did not support the taxpayer's characterization of the transaction as insurance). In Kidde Industries, Inc. v. United States, 40 Fed. Cl. 42 (1997), the United States Court of Federal Claims concluded that an arrangement between the captive insurance subsidiary and each of the 100 operating subsidiaries of the same parent constituted insurance for federal income tax purposes. As in Humana, the insurer in

Kidde insured only entities within its affiliated group during the taxable years at issue.

In the present case, the professional liability risks of 12 operating subsidiaries are shifted to S. Further, the premiums of the operating subsidiaries, determined at arms-length, are pooled such that a loss by one operating subsidiary is borne, in substantial part, by the premiums paid by others. The 12 operating subsidiaries and S conduct themselves in all respects as would unrelated parties to a traditional insurance relationship, and S is regulated as an insurance company in each state where it does business. The narrow question presented is whether P's common ownership of the 12 operating subsidiaries and S affects the conclusion that the arrangements at issue are insurance for federal income tax purposes. Under the facts presented, we conclude the arrangements between S and each of the 12 operating subsidiaries of S's parent constitute insurance for federal income tax purposes.

Holding

The amounts paid for professional liability coverage by the 12 domestic operating subsidiaries to S are "insurance premiums" deductible under § 162.

REVENUE RULE 2002-91

Internal Revenue Service (I.R.S.) Revenue Ruling

Captive insurance; Group captive

A revenue ruling that sets forth circumstances under which amounts paid to a group captive of unrelated insureds are deductible as insurance premiums.

A revenue ruling that sets forth circumstances under which a group captive of unrelated insureds qualifies as an insurance company.

(Also §§ 162, 801; 1.162-1, 1.801-3.)

Captive insurance; group captive. This ruling sets forth circumstances under which amounts paid to a group captive of unrelated insureds are deductible as insurance premiums and in which the group captive qualifies as an insurance company.

Issue

Whether a "group captive" formed by a relatively small group of unrelated businesses involved in a highly concentrated industry to provide insurance coverage is an insurance company within the meaning of § 831 of the Internal Revenue Code under the circumstances described below.

Facts

X is one of a small group of unrelated businesses involved in one highly concentrated industry. Businesses involved in this industry face significant liability hazards. X and the other businesses involved in this industry are required by regulators to maintain adequate liability insurance coverage in order to continue to operate. Businesses that participate in this industry have sustained significant losses due to the occurrence of unusually severe loss events. As a result, affordable insurance coverage for businesses that participate in this industry is not available from commercial insurance companies.

X and a significant number of the businesses involved in this industry (Members) form a so-called "group captive" (GC) to provide insurance coverage for stated liability risks. GC provides insurance only to X and the other Members. The business operations of GC are separate from the business operation of each Member. GC is adequately capitalized.

No Member owns more than 15% of GC, and no Member has more than 15% of the vote on any corporate governance issue. In addition, no Member's individual risk insured by GC exceeds 15% of the total risk insured by GC. Thus, no one member controls GC.

GC issues insurance contracts and charges premiums for the insurance coverage provided under the contracts. GC uses recognized actuarial techniques, based, in part, on commercial rates for similar coverage, to determine the premiums to be charged to an individual Member.

GC pools all the premiums it receives in its general funds and pays claims out of those funds. GC investigates any claim made by a Member to determine the validity of the claim prior to making any payment on that claim. GC conducts no other business than the issuing and administering of insurance contracts.

No Member has any obligation to pay GC additional premiums if that Member's actual losses during any period of coverage exceed the premiums paid by that Member. No Member will be entitled to a refund of premiums paid if that Member's actual losses are lower than the premiums paid for coverage during any period. Premiums paid by any Member may be used to satisfy claims of the other Members. No Member that terminates its insurance coverage or sells its ownership interest in GC is required to make additional premium or capital payments to GC to cover losses in excess of its premiums paid. Moreover, no Member that terminates its coverage or disposes of its ownership interest in GC is entitled to a refund of premiums paid in excess of insured losses.

Law and analysis

Section 162(a) of the Code provides, in part, that there shall be allowed as a deduction all the ordinary and necessary expenses paid or incurred during the taxable year in carrying on any trade or business.

Section 1.162-1(a) of the Income Tax Regulations provides, in part, that among the items included in business expenses are insurance premiums against fire, storms, theft, accident, or other similar losses in the case of a business.

Section 831(a) of the Code provides that taxes computed under section 11 are imposed for each tax year on the taxable income of every insurance company other than a life insurance company.

Section 1.801-3(a) provides that an insurance company is "a company whose primary and predominant business activity is the issuing of insurance or annuity contracts or the reinsuring of risks underwritten by insurance companies."

Neither the Code nor the regulations define the terms "insurance" or "insurance contract." The United States Supreme Court, however, has explained that in order for an arrangement to constitute insurance for federal income tax purposes, both risk shifting and risk distribution must be present. Helvering v. LeGierse, 312 U.S. 531 (1941).

Risk shifting occurs if a person facing the possibility of an economic loss transfers some or all of the financial consequences of the potential loss to the insurer, such that a loss by the insured does not affect the insured because the loss is offset by the insurance payment. Risk distribution incorporates the statistical phenomenon known as the law of large numbers. Distributing risk allows the insurer to reduce the possibility that a single costly claim will exceed the amount taken in as premiums and set aside for the payment of such a claim. By assuming numerous relatively small, independent risks that occur randomly over time, the insurer smooths out losses to match more closely its receipt of premiums. Clougherty Packing Co.

v. Commissioner, 811 F.2d 1297, 1300 (9th Cir. 1987). Risk distribution necessarily entails a pooling of premiums, so that a potential insured is not in significant part paying for its own risks. See Humana, Inc. v. Commissioner, 881 F.2d 247, 257 (6th Cir. 1989).

No court has held that a transaction between a parent and its wholly-owned subsidiary satisfies the requirements of risk shifting and risk distribution if only the risks of the parent are "insured." See Stearns-Roger Corp. v. United States, 774 F.2d 414 (10th Cir. 1985); Carnation Co. v. Commissioner, 640 F.2d 1010 (9th Cir. 1981), cert. denied, 454 U.S. 965 (1981). However, courts have held that an arrangement between a parent and its subsidiary can constitute insurance because the parent's premiums are pooled with those of unrelated parties if (i) insurance risk is present, (ii) risk is shifted and distributed, and (iii) the transaction is of the type that is insurance in the commonly accepted sense. See, e.g., Ocean Drilling & Exploration Co. v. United States, 988 F.2d 1135 (Fed. Cir. 1993); AMERCO, Inc. v. Commissioner, 979 F.2d 162 (9th Cir. 1992).

Additional factors to be considered in determining whether a captive insurance transaction is insurance include: whether the parties that insured with the captive truly face hazards; whether premiums charged by the captive are based on commercial rates; whether the validity of claims was established before payments are made; and whether the captive's business operations and assets are kept separate from the business operations and assets of its shareholders. Ocean Drilling & Exploration Co. at 1151.

In Rev. Rul. 2001-31, 2001-1 C.B.1348, the Service stated that it will not invoke the economic family theory in Rev. Rul. 77-316 with respect to captive insurance arrangements. Rev. Rul. 2001-31 provides, however, that the Service may continue to challenge certain captive insurance transactions based on the facts and circumstances of each case.

Rev. Rul. 78-338, 1978-2 C.B.107, presented a situation in which 31 unrelated corporations created a group captive insurance company to provide those corporations with insurance that was not otherwise available. In that ruling, none of the unrelated corporations held a controlling interest in the group captive. In addition, no individual corporation's risk exceeded 5 percent of the total risks insured by the group captive. The Service concluded that because the corporations that owned, and were insured by, the group captive were not economically related, the economic risk of loss could be shifted and distributed among the shareholders that comprised the insured group.

X and the other Members face true insurable hazards. X and the other Members are required to maintain general liability insurance coverage in order to continue to operate in their industry. X and the other Members are unable to obtain affordable insurance from unrelated commercial insurers due to the occurrence of unusually severe loss events. Notwithstanding the fact that the group of Members is small, there is a real possibility that a Member will sustain a loss in excess of the premiums it paid. No individual Member will be reimbursed for premiums paid in excess of losses sustained by that Member. Finally, X and the other Members are unrelated. Therefore, the contracts issued by GC to X and the other Members are insurance contracts for federal income tax purposes, and the premiums paid by the Members are deductible under § 162.

GC is an entity separate from its owners. GC is adequately capitalized. GC issues insurance contracts, charges premiums, and pays claims after investigating the validity of the claim. GC will not engage in any business activities other than issuing and administering insurance contracts. Premiums charged by GC will be actuarially determined using recognized actuarial techniques, and will be based, in part, on commercial rates. As GC's only business activity is the business of insurance, it is taxed as an insurance company.

Holding

The arrangement between X and GC constitutes insurance for federal income tax purposes, and the amounts paid as "insurance premiums" by X to GC pursuant to that arrangement are deductible as ordinary and necessary business expenses. GC is in the business of issuing insurance and will be treated as an insurance company taxable under § 831.

REVENUE RULE 2001-31

Captive insurance transactions

Section 118.—Contributions to the Capital of a Corporation, 26 CFR 1.118-1: Contributions to the capital of a corporation.

The revenue ruling obsoletes Rev. Rul. 77-316 (1977-2 C.B. 53), which provided that payments between related parties that were disallowed as deductions for insurance premiums should be recharacterized as contributions to capital under I.R.C. § 118.

Section 162.—Trade or Business Expenses, 26 CFR 1.162-1: Business expenses.

The revenue ruling announces that the Service will not raise the economic family theory, originally set forth in Rev. Rul. 77-316 (1977-2 C.B. 53), in determining whether payments between related parties are deductible insurance premiums.

Section 165.—Losses, 26 CFR 1.165-1: Losses.

The revenue ruling obsoletes Rev. Rul. 77-316 (1977-2 C.B. 53), which provided that losses paid by a captive insurance company pursuant to a related- party transaction deemed not to be insurance were deductible by the captive insurer's respective parent or affiliate under IRC § 165(a).

Section 301.—Distributions of Property, 26 CFR 1.301-1: Rules applicable with respect to distributions of money and other property.

The revenue ruling obsoletes Rev. Rul. 77-316 (1977-2 C.B. 53), which provided that losses paid by a captive insurance company pursuant to a related- party transaction deemed not to be insurance were viewed, to the extent of available earnings and profits, as distributions under IRC § 301 to the respective parent.

Section 801.—Tax Imposed, 26 CFR 1.801-3: Definitions.

The revenue ruling obsoletes Rev. Rul. 77-316 (1977-2 C.B. 53), which provided that certain captive insurance companies were not taxable as insurance companies pursuant to IRC §§ 801, 831, and the applicable regulations because the related-party transactions could not be considered "insurance" for purposes of determining whether the captive insurer was "primarily and predominantly engaged in the insurance business," as required in Treas. Reg. § 1.801-3(a).

Section 831.—Tax on Insurance Companies Other Than Life Insurance Companies, 26 CFR 1.831-3: Tax on insurance companies (other than life or mutual), mutual marine insurance companies, mutual fire insurance companies issuing perpetual policies, and mutual fire or flood insurance companies operating on the basis of premium deposits; taxable years beginning after December 31, 1962.

The revenue ruling obsoletes Rev. Rul. 77-316 (1977-2 C.B. 53), which provided that certain captive insurance companies were not taxable as insurance companies pursuant to IRC §§ 801, 831, and the applicable regulations because the related-party transactions could not be considered "insurance" for purposes of determining whether the captive insurer was "primarily and predominantly engaged in the insurance business," as required in Treas. Reg. § 1.801-3(a).

26 CFR 1.162-1: Business expenses.

Captive insurance transactions. This ruling explains that the Service will no longer raise the "economic family theory," set forth in Rev. Rul. 77-316 (1977-2 C.B. 53), in addressing whether captive insurance transactions constitute valid insurance. Rather, the Service will address captive insurance transactions on a case-by-case basis. Rev. Ruls. 77-316, 78-277, 88-72, and 89-61 obsoleted. Rev. Ruls. 78-338, 80-120, 92-93, and 2000-3 modified.

This ruling explains that the Service will no longer raise the "economic family theory" set forth in Rev. Rul. 77-316 (1977-2 C.B. 53), in addressing whether captive insurance transactions constitute valid insurance. Rather, the Service will address captive insurance transactions on a case-by-case basis.

In Rev. Rul. 77-316 (1977-2 C.B. 53), three situations were presented in which a taxpayer attempted to seek insurance coverage for itself and its operating subsidiaries through the taxpayer's wholly-owned captive insurance subsidiary. The ruling explained that the taxpayer, its non-insurance subsidiaries, and its captive insurance subsidiary represented one "economic family" for purposes of analyzing whether transactions involved sufficient risk shifting and risk distribution to constitute insurance for federal income tax purposes. See Helvering v. Le Gierse, 312 U.S. 531 (1941). The ruling concluded that the transactions were not insurance to the extent that risk was retained within that economic family. Therefore, the premiums paid by the taxpayer and its non-insurance subsidiaries to the captive insurer were not deductible.

No court, in addressing a captive insurance transaction, has fully accepted the economic family theory set forth in Rev. Rul. 77-316. See, e.g., Humana, Inc. v. Commissioner, 881 F.2d 247 (6th Cir. 1989); Clougherty Packing Co. v. Commissioner, 811 F.2d 1297 (9th Cir. 1987) (employing a balance sheet test, rather than the economic family theory, to conclude that transaction between parent and subsidiary was not insurance); Kidde Industries, Inc. v. United States, 40 Fed. Cl. 42 (1997). Accordingly, the Internal Revenue Service will no longer invoke the economic family theory with respect to captive insurance transactions.

The Service may, however, continue to challenge certain captive insurance transactions based on the facts and circumstances of each case. See, e.g., Malone & Hyde v. Commissioner, 62 F.3d 835 (6th Cir. 1995) (concluding that brother-sister transactions were not insurance because the taxpayer guaranteed the captive's performance and the captive was thinly capitalized and loosely regulated); Clougherty Packing Co. v. Commissioner (concluding that a transaction between parent and subsidiary was not insurance).

REVENUE RULE 92-93

Internal Revenue Service Revenue Ruling

Insurance Subsidiary Insuring Its Parent Corporations Employees

Published: November 9, 1992

Section 79. Group-Term Life Insurance Purchased for Employees, 26 CFR 1.79-1: Group-term life insurance.

(See Also Sections 61, 162; 1.61 2, 1.162 1.)

Insurance subsidiary insuring its parent corporation's employees. Except for the cost of $50,000 of insurance coverage, each employee of a parent corporation must include in gross income under section 79 of the Code an amount equal to the cost of group-term life insurance on the employee's life purchased by the parent from its wholly owned insurance subsidiary. Parent may deduct the premiums paid to the insurance subsidiary for the group-term life insurance on an employee of the parent. Rev.Ruls. 77-316 and 88-72 distinguished.

Issues

1. If a parent corporation carries insurance on its employees' lives under a group-term life insurance contract purchased from the parent's wholly owned insurance subsidiary, may the employees exclude from gross income under section 79 of the Internal Revenue Code an amount equal to the cost of $50,000 of the life insurance coverage?

2. Are payments to be made by a parent corporation to its wholly owned insurance subsidiary for group-term life insurance coverage for the parent's employees deductible under section 162 of the Code?

Facts

X, a domestic manufacturing corporation whose stock is widely held, obtains for each of its employees $100,000 of life insurance coverage under a nonparticipating group-term life insurance contract. The employees do not reimburse X or pay any of the cost of the coverage. X is not a direct or indirect beneficiary under the contract, and the proceeds of the contract are payable to the employees' beneficiaries.

The contract is issued to X by S1, a wholly owned insurance subsidiary of X. S1 is engaged in the trade or business of issuing life insurance and annuity contracts to the general public. S1 is regulated as an insurance company by the states where it transacts business. The contract issued to X qualifies as a life insurance contract under applicable state law. The contractual terms, including the premium rates, are customary in the industry. There is no guarantee of a renewal of the contract by S1. No permanent benefits (for example, a cash surrender value) are provided under the contract.

Law and analysis

Issue 1

Section 61(a) of the Code provides that gross income includes compensation for services, which includes fringe benefits.

Section 1.61-1(a) of the Income Tax Regulations states that gross income means all income realized from whatever source derived, unless excluded by law. Gross income includes income realized in any form, whether in money, property, or services.

Section 1.61-2(d)(1) of the regulations states that if services are paid for in property, the fair market value of the property taken in payment must be included in income as compensation.

Section 1.61-2(d)(2)(ii) of the regulations states that life insurance premiums paid by an employer on the life of an employee where the proceeds of the insurance are payable to the beneficiary of the employee generally are part of the gross income of the employee. Special rules under section 79 of the Code, however, govern the includibility in an employee's gross income of group- term life insurance carried directly or indirectly by his or her employer on the employee's life. See also section 83(e)(5) (section 83 inapplicable to group-term life insurance to which section 79 applies).

Section 79(a) of the Code provides that there shall be included in the gross income of an employee for the taxable year an amount equal to the cost of group-term life insurance on the employee's life for part or all of such year under a policy (or policies) carried directly or indirectly by an employer to the extent that such cost exceeds the sum of (1) the cost of $50,000 of such insurance, and (2) the amount (if any) paid by the employee toward the purchase of such insurance.

Insurance requires the shifting of an economic risk of loss from the insured to the insurer. Helvering v. Le Gierse, 312 U.S. 531 (1941), 1941-1 C.B. 430. Risk shifting entails the transfer of a potential loss from the insured to the insurer. Rev.Rul. 77-316, 1977-2 C.B. 53, as amplified and clarified by Rev.Rul. 88-72, 1988-2 C.B. 31, as clarified by Rev.Rul. 89-61, 1989-1 C.B. 75, concludes that risk shifting does not exist under arrangements whereby a parent corporation purports to shift a risk of the parent to its wholly owned insurance subsidiary. The ruling explains:

[T]he insuring parent corporation and its domestic subsidiaries, and the wholly owned "insurance" subsidiary, though separate corporate entities, represent one economic family with the result that those who bear the ultimate economic burden of loss are the same persons who suffer the loss.

1977-2 C.B. at 54.

Although X purchased the group-term life insurance contract covering its employees from its wholly owned insurance subsidiary, S1, this fact does not cause the arrangement to be "self-insurance" because the economic risk of loss being insured shifted to S1 is not a risk of X.

The group-term life insurance that X provides to its employees is compensation for the performance of services. In partial consideration for the employees' services, X paid the premium on a contract that provides each employee with $100,000 of term life insurance coverage. This insurance on the employees' lives is an economic benefit to the employees since it relieves them of the expense of providing life insurance for themselves. Unless excluded under the Code, the value of insurance provided X's employees in connection with the performance of services is includible in the employees' gross income. Section 1.61-2(d)(2)(ii) of the regulations. Therefore, in accordance with section 79 and the regulations thereunder, each employee of X may exclude from gross income an amount equal to the cost of $50,000 of the group-term life insurance carried by X on the employee's life. The cost of insurance coverage in excess of $50,000 must be included in the employee's gross income.

Issue 2

Section 162(a) of the Code provides that there shall be allowed as a deduction all the ordinary and necessary expenses paid or incurred during the taxable year in carrying on any trade or business, including a reasonable allowance for salaries or other compensation for personal services actually rendered.

Section 1.162-1(a) of the regulations states that among the items included in business expenses are labor expenses.

Section 264(a)(1) of the Code provides that no deduction is allowed for premiums paid on any life insurance policy covering the life of any officer or employee, or of any person financially interested in any trade or business carried on by the taxpayer, when the taxpayer is directly or indirectly a beneficiary under such policy.

The amounts paid by X to S1 for group-term life insurance are part of the compensation for the employees' services. If an employer augments an employee's salary by paying the premiums on the employee's life insurance, the premiums are deductible business expenses provided the aggregate amount of compensation does not exceed reasonable compensation for the employee's services and provided the employer is not directly or indirectly a beneficiary under the policy. See Rev.Rul. 56-400, 1956-2 C.B. 116. The holding of Rev.Rul. 77-316 does not preclude an employer from deducting the cost of insurance coverage provided employees as additional compensation for their services in this case because the arrangement in this case does not involve self-insurance. Cf. section 1.809-5(a)(12) of the regulations (allowing a life insurance company a deduction for amounts representing premiums that the company charges itself with respect to liability for employee insurance and annuity benefits). Accordingly, if the aggregate amount of compensation for an employee's services does not exceed reasonable compensation for the employee's services, X may deduct the premiums paid to S1 for the group-term life insurance on that employee. But see Gulf Oil Corp. v. Commissioner, 89 T.C. 1010 (1987), aff'd, 914 F.2d 396 (3rd Cir.1990) (no deduction allowed to parent corporation for amounts paid for waiver of premium coverage for disabled employees under a group life insurance plan). The Internal Revenue Service will not follow the decision in Gulf Oil to the extent that it denies a deduction for amounts a parent corporation pays to shift risks of unrelated employees and their beneficiaries to the parent's wholly owned insurance subsidiary.

Holdings

1. If a parent corporation carries insurance on its employees' lives under a group-term life insurance contract purchased from the parent's wholly owned insurance subsidiary, the employees may exclude from gross income under section 79 of the Code an amount equal to the cost of $50,000 of the life insurance coverage.

2. X may deduct the premiums paid to S1 for group-term life insurance on X's employees provided the aggregate amount of compensation with respect to each employee is reasonable.

Application

The holdings of this revenue ruling also apply to accident and health insurance. Thus, unless excluded under the Code, the value of the accident and health insurance (including waiver of premium coverage upon disability) provided by an employer to its employees in connection with the performance of services is compensation includible in the employees' gross income under section 61 of the Code. The employer may deduct the premiums paid to its wholly owned insurance subsidiary for accident and health insurance on an employee provided the aggregate amount of compensation to the employee does not exceed reasonable compensation.

Appendix C: Captive Insurance Company Formation Timeline

Following is an outline of a typical timeline for the formation of a captive insurance company. Your experience may be different depending on the complexity of your captive and the businesses and risks it insures.

Captive Formation Timeline		
Action Step	Time	Responsibility
Complete or finalize Actuarial Report including pure loss cost, expected and adverse scenarios and premium rate study.	2 Weeks	Client provides exposure measures to the actuary. Attorney consults policy language, what will be covered, what will be excluded.
		Actuary finalizes report
Prepare and file Articles and Bylaws in domicile of formation		Captive manager
Draft Policies to be issued by Captive		Attorney
Prepare five-year pro forma financial Statements using final actuarial report	1 Week	CPA for the captive drafts proforma. Consults with captive manager and actuary for capitalization and premium levels.
Draft letter supporting capitalization projections on both a suspected and adverse basis	1-2 Days	Actuary
Draft captive business plan	1 Week	Captive manager
Complete captive application for domicile of formatio		
Submit captive application and business plan to regulators for approval.		
Application is reviewed by captive insurance commissioner and staff	3-4 Weeks	Captive manager consults with regulators on questions regarding the submission. Other service providers are available as needed to answer specific questions
Application is approved	1-2 Weeks	Captive manager advises captive owners of approval and coordinates submission of taxes and fees
Initial premium taxes and fees are submitted		
Captive establishes bank account and funds initial capital and paid in surplus		Captive manager works with bank(er) to establish account, owner funds capital
Captive is operational		

Appendix D: Feasibility Study Outline

Feasibility Study: A captive feasibility study should adhere to the following format:

A. Cover Page: The cover page should include the name of the captive insurance company, the names, addresses and telephone numbers for each individual involved in preparing the study, and the date of the report.

B. Background and Scope of the Analysis: While the order, language and format is left to the individuals preparing the study, this section should include:

1. Identification of the parent or members of the proposed captive,
2. Statement of why the study was undertaken,
3. Summary of coverage, policy forms, lines of business, limits, deductibles, and retentions,
4. Summary of source of funds (i.e. premiums, LOC accessibility, etc.)

C. Summary of Recommendations: This summary should contain the basic findings and conclusions as well as the key assumptions underlying those findings and conclusions. The following specific information should be included:

1. Discussion of rates, rate structure, and premium level broken out by line of insurance,
2. Discussion of the degree of capitalization and the level of confidence in the aggregate funding, which should include premiums and investment income.
3. In the case of an association captive, a discussion of the minimum number of participants required to form a critical mass that makes the program feasible,
4. Summary of results of pro forma financial statements, including a worse than expected scenario demonstrating

the possibility of serious financial loss or impairment.

D. Analysis Section: Where analysis sections, as listed above, have been omitted, are not relevant, or are not required, their absence from the feasibility study should be noted. Each section is further described as follows:

1. *Data analysis* should include studies based on estimates of expected frequency and severity of loss using available data. These estimates may be derived from: trended and developed historical loss data; outside sources of data (ISO, RAA, etc....); expertise within the firm; and judgment. It should be noted, however, that judgmental estimates should be disclosed as such and the source clearly stated. Judgmental estimates may be accepted as long as they are clearly disclosed.

2. *Loss projections and risk margins* of expected and higher-than-expected levels of loss should be included. These projections and margins are either actuarially determined and states as such or the methodology used is clearly documented. In all loss projection sections, each step should be explained in terms of how and why the procedure was used. For example, how is trend and loss development handled? Are losses discounted?

3. *Expense budget* for the captive insurance company should be clearly discussed. In addition, the study must make reference to tax issues. The tax issues should address, either the state that the captive is subject to within the models, or that the captive insurance company is not subject to taxes consequences. Should the study state that the captive is not subject to taxes of certain jurisdictions the reasons for this must be clearly documented. The Department considers tax consequences to be an extremely important consideration of captive formation. Types of tax issues may include but are not limited to the following:

a) U.S. Income Taxes (with respect to the captive and to owners)
b) Excise Taxes
c) Excess and Surplus Lines Taxes
d) Domicile Premium Taxes (Utah does not have premium taxes – only an annual fee of $5,000)
e) Other assessments or applicable taxes

4. *Premiums/Funding* items (2) and (3) should be brought together in order to develop the total recommended premium for the captive.

5. *Capitalization* is needed to cover the variability and uncertainty of expected loss levels. Therefore, a relatively extensive discussion of capitalization should be included in the study. Included in the discussion should be a review of minimum participation requirements and any heuristic logic used in determining capitalization.

E. Pro Forma Financial Statement: Pro forma financial models should include the following items:

1. An income statement and balance sheet
2. Parameters which agree with the other analyses in the study
3. At least 3 years of pro forma results (unless long tail business which takes longer to develop then provide sufficient years to show projected or expected development).
4. At least one scenario worse than expected which demonstrates the consideration of possible financial impairment.
5. Detailed explanation of each modeling assumption.
6. General assumptions such as interest rates, year-to-year growth rates, etc.
7. Model showing the minimum number of participants, premiums, or capital.

F. <u>Other Sections:</u> In order to add value to the study, the "other sections" should be used to describe other areas of the captive in which standards have not yet been developed. These areas may include, but are not limited to, the following:

1. Fronting
2. Rating
3. Dividend, or profit allocation policy
4. Capital allocation, alternative captive techniques
5. Accessibility

Appendix E: Sample License Application

Application to form a captive insurance company in Utah

General information section:

1. Proposed Name of the Captive Insurance Company.

2. Company Name of Parent(s) or Sponsor(s) of the Proposed Captive:

Parent(s)/Sponsor(s) Net Worth:	$
Parent(s)/Sponsor(s) Information	
Name:	
Street Address:	
City, State, Zip:	
Telephone No.:	
Email Address:	

Please Describe the Relationship of the Parent(s)/Sponsor(s) to each other and the Proposed Captive Insurer.

3. Individual to be Contacted regarding this Application

Name:	
Street Address:	
City, State, Zip:	
Telephone No.:	
Email Address:	
Cell Phone/Pager:	

4. Type of Captive being Proposed
    (Check the appropriate type)

Pure	▨	Association	▨	Industrial Sponsored	▨
Branch	▨	Sponsored	▨		

5. Organization Type of Proposed Captive:

Stock	▨	Mutual	▨	Reciprocal	▨

6. Address and Location of Principal Office/Place of Business
    of Proposed Captive:

7. Name and Address of Registered Agent for Service of
    Process:

Name:	
Street Address:	
City, State, Zip:	
Telephone No.:	
Email Address:	
Cell Phone/Pager:	

8. Location Where Books and Records of Captive will be
   Kept:

Street Address:	
City, State, Zip:	
Telephone No.:	
Email Address:	

9. Names of Board of Directors of Proposed Captive:
   *(Biographical Affidavits must be provided for each
   director. Please use the department's biographical
   affidavit form.)*

10. Names of Officers of the Proposed Captive:
    *(Biographical Affidavits must be provided for each
    office. Please use the department's biographical
    affidavit form.)*

President	
Vice President	
Secretary	
Treasurer	

Financial information section:

1. Capitalization (if Stock Captive Selected)

a. Amount of Paid-In-Capital	$
b. Type of Stock to be Authorized	Number of Shares
(1)	
(2)	
c. Par Value of Stock Shares by Type	Selling Price
(1)	$
(2)	$

2. Funding of Mutual or Reciprocal Captive

Amount of Contributed Surplus	$

3. Proposed Capitalization in the Form of Letters of Credit:
   (Please provide the following information relating to the letters of credit. The Utah Letter of Credit Form must be furnished with this application.)(If more than one LOC is utilized Provide the following on a separate sheet.)

Types of LOC:	
Amount of LOC:	
Issued in Favor of:	
Name of Bank	
Street Address of Bank	
City, State, Zip of Bank	

4. Capital and Surplus of Captive

Initial Capital	$
Initial Surplus	$
Total Capital and Surplus	$
Location of Shares of Stock	

5. Name(s) and Address(es) of Beneficial Owners

Name:	
Street Address:	
City, State, Zip	
Ownership Percentage:	

Name:	
Street Address:	
City, State, Zip	
Ownership Percentage:	

Name:	
Street Address:	
City, State, Zip	
Ownership Percentage:	

Name:	
Street Address:	
City, State, Zip	
Ownership Percentage:	

6. Describe the relationship between the beneficial owners.

Service providers section:

1. Name and Address of Management Firm (If applicable)

Name:	
Street Address:	
City, State, Zip	
Telephone:	
E-mail Address:	
Contact Person:	

2. Name and Address of Attorney

Name:	
Street Address:	
City, State, Zip	
Telephone:	
E-mail Address:	
Contact Person:	

3. Name and Address of Claims Administrator

Name:	
Street Address:	
City, State, Zip	
Telephone:	
E-mail Address:	
Contact Person:	

4. Name and Address of Certified Public Accountant

Name:	
Street Address:	
City, State, Zip	
Telephone:	
E-mail Address:	
Contact Person:	

5. Name and Address of Actuary

Name:	
Street Address:	
City, State, Zip	
Telephone:	
E-mail Address:	
Contact Person:	

6. Name and address of Insurance Broker

Name:	
Street Address:	
City, State, Zip	
Telephone:	
E-mail Address:	
Contact Person:	

7. If this application is related to an Industrial Insured Captive, please provide the following:

   a. Name and address of each full-time employee acting as an Insurance Manager or buyer.

   b. Aggregate annual Premium Amount: $

   c. Number of full-time employees:

Miscellaneous information and attachments section:

1. Please include the following information with this
   application:

   a. An explanation of insurance coverage /limits/
      reinsurance. [Use the Utah Insurance Department
      Captive Insurance Company Reinsurance Exhibit
      (Coverage/Limits/Reinsurance) Form]

   b. A certified copy of the Captive's charter, certificate
      of incorporation, articles of incorporation and bylaws
      or if being formed as a reciprocal, a certified copy of
      the power of attorney-in-fact and subscriber's agree-
      ment. Certified copies of these documents must be
      filed before a certificate of authority is issued.

   c. A non-refundable application fee of $200.

   d. A feasibility study prepared by a qualified,
      independent actuary,

   e. A statement of benefit to State of Utah (Certificate of
      Public Good).

   f. Biographical affidavits for all officers and directors of
      the proposed captive insurer.

   g. If applicant is an Association Captive, please give a
      history, purpose, size and other details of the parent
      association.

   List all other providers and their responsibilities together
   with how fees for services rendered are to be charged.

   h. A detailed business plan of operations with support-
      ing data including:

      1) Risks to be insured (direct, indirect, assumed,
         and ceded by line of business);
      2) Fronting company if operating as a reinsurer;

3) Expected net annual premium income;
4) Maximum retained risk (per loss and annual aggregate);
5) Rating program;
6) Reinsurance program;
7) Organization and responsibility for loss prevention and safety including the main procedures followed and steps taken to deal with events prior to possible claims;
8) Loss Experience for past three years together with projections for next three years of operations;
9) An organizational chart; and
10) Financial projections on an expected and worse claims scenario.

j. The annual report for the parent

k. 10K or personal financial statements of owners

(Items (a) though (k) above are to be submitted in a three-ring notebook with numbered and lettered tabs with the required information immediately following each tab. The information in the business plan relating to items i(1), i(3), i(4), and i(10) should be projected for a three-year period.)

Appendix F: Elliot Spitzer's Testimony to the United States Senate

STATE OF NEW YORK ATTORNEY GENERAL
ELIOT SPITZER
TESTIMONY UNITED STATES SENATE
COMMITTEE ON GOVERNMENTAL AFFAIRS

SUBCOMMITTEE ON FINANCIAL MANAGEMENT,
THE BUDGET AND INTERNATIONAL SECURITY

Washington, D.C.
November 16, 2004

Introduction

Over the last year, my Office has undertaken an investigation into the market practices of insurance brokers. Insurance brokers serve businesses and individuals seeking to purchase insurance, and they hold strict fiduciary duties to serve the best interests of their clients. We were concerned that brokers were subject to conflicts of interest due to their receipt of contingent commissions and other hidden payments from certain insurance companies for steering client business to preferred insurers. Very quickly, our investigation found widespread evidence that brokers were receiving hidden payments, essentially kickbacks, from insurance companies.

By looking closely at these contingent commissions, we uncovered another side of the insurance industry. Not only do insurance brokers receive contingent commissions to steer business, but many brokers, with the assistance and collusion of insurance companies, engage in systematic fraud and market manipulation in order to ensure that profitable and high volume business goes to a few selected insurance companies. In other words, we found that favoritism, secrecy and conflicts rule this market, and not open competition.

This struck us as a very familiar pattern. Whether in investigating conflicts of interest between the research and investment banking arms of large Wall Street firms or our recent work in the mutual fund industry, we have found that the lack of transparency, combined with inadequate disclosure and regulatory oversight, often leads to market fraud and collusion. Many insurance lines, from employee benefits to property and casualty, essentially function as insiders' clubs, where those with market clout and power pay for preferential treatment. Similar to the small investor on Wall Street or in mutual funds, the ordinary purchaser of insurance has no idea that the broker he selects is receiving hidden payments from insurance companies, that the advice he receives from the broker may be compromised, or that the market bids he sees may be illusory. This has led to a crisis of accountability.

Industry Background

The insurance industry is vast, and touches nearly every segment of the national economy. Insurance companies wrote a net total of approximately $1.1 trillion in premium in 2003, or approximately 10 cents of every dollar of the $11 trillion Gross Domestic Product. Even minor variations in premium pricing have dramatic consequences on the economy.

Much of this industry, however, operates in secrecy. Under the McCarran-Ferguson Act of 1945, 15 U.S.C. § 1011 et seq., the regulation of insurance is delegated almost entirely to the States. Disclosure laws among the States, however, vary. Furthermore, an increasing number of insurers and brokers maintain offshore operations, particularly in Bermuda.

In addition, market power in the insurance brokerage market has rapidly consolidated over the last ten years. A market study conducted by Swiss Re found that in 2002 Marsh and AON together comprised 54 percent of the global brokerage market, and Willis comprises an additional 7 percent. These two or three firms also dominate reinsurance brokerage markets.

With so much market power concentrated in two or three brokerage firms, the threat of collusion has become a reality. We found that a small group of brokers and insurance companies essentially control the market, having created a network of interlocking connections and secret payments which ensure that the bulk of business goes to certain insurers and that profits remain high. The bottom line is that the consumer pays more for coverage.

1. Marsh & McLennan
On October 14, 2004, my Office filed a complaint against Marsh & McLennan Companies and Marsh Inc., alleging widespread fraud and antitrust violations in the procurement and broking of insurance. Many of the nation's largest insurance companies were implicated in these practices, including American International Group ("AIG"), ACE Ltd., and The Hartford Financial Services Group.

Concurrent with the Marsh action, my office filed two criminal complaints against executives at AIG, charging a scheme to defraud in violation of New York State Penal Law §
190.65 and a third criminal complaint against an executive at ACE, charging violation of New York State antitrust law under General Business Law § 340. All three executives pleaded guilty.

2. Universal Life Resources, Inc.
Last Friday, my Office filed a complaint against Universal Life Resources, Inc. ("ULR"), a key consultant and broker in the employee benefits industry. ULR advises hundreds of employers in the selection of insurance and has placed insurance for four million U.S. workers. The complaint details how ULR

is retained to help employers reduce costs and procure the most appropriate benefit plans for their employees, but instead engages in massive steering of this business to a small set of insurers that have been willing to enter into side-deals with lucrative payoffs for ULR. These insurers include Unum Provident Insurance Company, Metropolitan Life Insurance Company and Prudential Financial Corporation. It is, of course, employees who pay for these hidden costs through higher life and other group premiums.

Summary of Investigation and Findings
Many purchasers of insurance, whether corporations or individuals, use independent insurance brokers for assistance in sorting through the numerous insurance products available and to obtain the best available coverage at the lowest price. Although these brokers have a fiduciary duty of loyalty to serve their clients' best interests faithfully, we found these duties are systematically betrayed by brokers with the aid of the insurance carriers.

All insurance brokers receive compensation when they obtain insurance for their clients. Typically, this compensation takes the form of a customary 10 percent commission paid by the insurance company out of the client's first premium check. However, some insurance clients forego this arrangement and pay their brokers a direct fee.

Our investigation revealed that in addition to this customary disclosed commission, many brokers also receive contingent compensation from insurance companies based on the volume and/or profitability of the business that the broker places with them. These payments are known as "contingent commissions," but go my many other names such as "overrides," or in the case of Marsh, placement service agreements ("PSAs") or market service agreements ("MSAs").

We found that brokers routinely mislead their clients about the true nature of contingent commissions. Marsh's website, for instance, described MSAs as "agreements that cover payment for the value brokers provide to insurance carriers." The truth is that contingent commissions and MSAs provide little or no value or services to insurance carriers. They appear to be nothing more than payments for steering business to preferred insurance carriers.

We were concerned about the obvious conflicts of interest that arise when insurance intermediaries have undisclosed incentives to "steer" business to certain insurance carriers in return for additional compensation. However, we did not anticipate the sheer magnitude of this practice, or how these hidden payments drive the insurance business as a whole. We have found:

- Contingent commissions plays an important role in the business models of many insurance brokers. Marsh established a separate business unit solely for the purpose of negotiating, collecting and extracting contingent commissions.
- Contingent commissions are highly profitable: for example, in 2003, Marsh received $845 million in such payments, and because little or no service is performed for steering business to insurance carriers, this $845 million represents almost pure profit.
- Smaller insurance brokers also enter into contingent commission agreements with insurance companies for the purpose of steering business.
- Many of the major insurance companies have entered into contingent commission agreements with brokers, and are paying millions of dollars in additional commissions, which contributes to rising premiums.
- Contingent commissions have infected practically every line of insurance business we examined, including employee benefits, medical malpractice, property, casualty, excess and surplus lines, executive risk, personal lines, marine, and aviation.

Contingent commissions also infect the reinsurance markets, which is a major cost driver for retail insurance costs and premiums. Reinsurance is insurance purchased by insurance companies to cover the risk created by the retail insurance policies they underwrite. In investigating this area, we found that the large retail insurance brokers also dominate the reinsurance brokerage market, and they have found numerous and creative ways to get second, third and fourth bites at the undisclosed compensation apple through reinsurance.

Contingent commissions represent the first source of undisclosed or poorly disclosed income. However, in exchange for entering into contingent commissions and steering retail insurance to an insurance carrier, brokers sometimes demand that the carrier enter into a reciprocal relationship to use the broker for the carrier's reinsurance purchases, resulting in additional reinsurance commissions to the broker. This represents a second source of undisclosed income. Essentially, brokers agree to an undisclosed quid pro quo with insurers: we'll steer more retail business to the insurance carrier if the carrier uses our reinsurance brokerage services. This arrangement results in significant undisclosed income and creates new conflicts of interest for retail brokers seeking to lock-in reinsurance commissions.

If the broker places reinsurance with a reinsurance carrier, the broker receives a customary disclosed commission and may also receive additional undisclosed income as a result of maintaining a contingent commission with reinsurance companies. This constitutes a possible third bite at undisclosed earnings. Finally, some brokers manage a fourth bite at the apple through maintaining investments in reinsurance companies to which they steer the reinsurance business.

Thus, across the entire life span of an insurable risk, brokers may receive as many as four additional streams of income in addition to receiving customary retail commissions. All of these payments, however, are undisclosed, or poorly disclosed, and place higher costs on the insurance itself, resulting in higher premium payments by consumers.

Contingent commissions and side-dealings between brokers and insurance companies also distort competition by turning insurance markets into an insiders' club, where business is steered to a select few insurance carriers who are willing to pay for these opportunities. Those carriers who enter into these agreements with brokers are usually assured that they will become a "partner" or a "favored nation," which are euphemisms for getting preferential, and sometimes criminal favoritism. Those carriers who refuse to "pay to play" are disciplined by seeing their premiums drop as brokers steer business to other carriers.

To make the system work, however, the broker has to deliver the promised volume of business to the insurance company that is paying it to steer. This pressure to deliver business leads brokers to engage in bid rigging and other forms of market manipulation. We found:

- Evidence of direct bid rigging in excess casualty insurance markets where Marsh arranged for the submission of fictitious or artificially inflated bids in order to create the illusion of competition among insurance carriers and mask the direct steering of insurance business to a favored insurance carrier. Criminal charges were filed against two AIG employees and one ACE employee in connection with this scheme.
- Cases where Marsh arranged for insurance carriers to refrain from bidding on certain accounts in order to limit competition and steer business to a preferred carrier.
- Evidence of proposed or actual "no shopping" agreements where Marsh and ULR would affirmatively undertake not to shop policies when they come up for renewal, essentially guaranteeing that the business stayed with the incumbent insurer.

• Numerous indirect examples of steering such as brokers offering favored carriers opportunities to be the lowest bidder but not offering similar opportunities to other bidders.

Significance of Findings

We have identified two major adverse impacts arising from these practices. First, steering results in strong incentives for the broker to send insurance business to preferred insurance companies which means that the customer is not always getting the best coverage for its needs. Second, the interlocking network of insurance brokers and insurance carriers essentially creates a secret cartel based on hidden payments and preferential treatment. Like any cartel, however, this one results in higher prices for the public and a drag on the economy. This causes inefficiencies and ultimately higher costs in a sector amounting to 10 percent of the national economy.

Reform and the Next Step

My Office intends to follow its investigation to its natural conclusion. We have sued Marsh and ULR and are continuing our investigation of collusion and fraud between brokers and insurers. We have also begun to look at other troubling areas of the insurance industry beyond steering and bid rigging. However, there are limits to what this Office can do. The problems we have uncovered in the insurance industry are profound, complicated and national in scope. We represent the interests of only one State and cannot unilaterally accomplish the systemic nationwide reform that is urgently needed.

Here are some areas warranting further investigation:

1. The Trend Offshore

One area that requires close attention is the extent to which insurance brokers and insurance companies have sought to evade State regulation by locating their operations in Bermuda and other offshore havens. This makes the States' job of supervising these companies far more difficult and creates numerous opportunities for secrecy and insider dealings.

Since 2001, there has been a reported huge transfer of insurance capital and underwriting activity to Bermuda, and more recently the Cayman Islands. Many of these off-shore entities are either owned in part or operated by the insurance brokers themselves. Marsh helped to create the Bermuda-based Ace Ltd., XL Capital Ltd., Mid Ocean Re and Axis, while AON has sponsored LaSalle Re and Endurance. This sets the stage for conflicts of interest, steering and self-dealing in insurance and reinsurance markets that we are just beginning to understand. And this is not to mention the numerous and profound tax implications of permitting U.S. insurers to accrue investment earnings in favorable offshore havens.

2. Antitrust Issues

Second, we believe we have only scratched the surface with regard to the interlocking relationships between insurance companies and between brokers and insurance companies that affect pricing and market competition. This is an industry that has traditionally been exempted from broad areas of federal and state antitrust laws. Broker rigging of markets is one manner in which premium costs stay high, but we believe there are other means by which brokers coordinate pricing such as setting prices through rate service organizations and trade associations, which serve as clearing houses for the setting and publishing of price information.

3. Disclosure on Premiums

A third and related area for investigation is the setting of premiums themselves, which remains a mysterious function. What percent of premium actually goes toward paying claims as opposed to simply being invested for income? In 2003, property and casualty insurers netted $38.7 billion in investment income, constituting by far the largest component of earnings for the year. With investments comprising the lion's share of insurance company earnings, we need to ask ourselves to what extent are investment performance and interest rates driving premiums and what manner of disclo-

sure is appropriate here, so that consumers of insurance understand why they are paying the rates they do?

4. Insurance Culture and Ethics
   Lastly, the brokers should be called to account for their steering activities. How has the culture of favoritism and pay-offs
   distorted their basic fiduciary duty to serve the customer.
   More importantly, how can we take steps to reform this culture by requiring appropriate disclosure to ensure the markets are operating properly?

Conclusion
From our work in this area, it is clear that the federal government's hands-off policy with regard to insurance combined
with uneven State-regulation has not entirely worked. There
are too many gaps in regulation across the 50 states and many
state regulators have not been sufficiently aggressive in terms
of supervising this industry.

The federal government should not preempt state insurance en-
forcement and regulation. Nonetheless, I do believe there is a
role for the federal government, especially in the areas of offshore capitalization and investment by insurance companies. At
a minimum, federal involvement may be necessary to assure
some basic standards of accountability on the part of insurance
professionals.

Congress has acted in similar cases. Whether in investigating
and implementing reforms for the oil and railroad cartels of
the late 19th century, or more recent probes into the savings
and loan industry, tobacco, or energy markets and Enron Corp.,
there is ample precedent for Congress to investigate the insurance industry and to undertake reform. In fact, in 1991, the
House Energy and Commerce Committee examined this industry in light of a rash of insurance company insolvencies,
and concluded that State law did not adequately ensure the financial integrity of insurers or punish insurers for violation of
State insurance laws. I believe further Congressional action

would go a long way toward avoiding the type of business dysfunction and collapse that has characterized other industries in recent years, and would be a first step toward controlling soaring insurance prices for the American consumer.

[i] *Why Go Captive? Increase Control, Reduce Costs.* http://www.vermontcaptive.com/basics/whyvermont.cfm (accessed September 14, 2007).

[ii] *Id.*

[iii] Kranish, Michael. 2003. For Dean, "captive" insurance a Vt. Boon. *Boston Globe*, December 13, sec. A.

[iv] Ariz. Rev. Stat. Ann.§ 20-1098.01(B)(3) (2002).

[v] *The New Captive Insurance Legislation Complements State Economic Development Effort.* http://www.doi.sc.gov/Eng/Public/Captives/WhySC.aspx (accessed August 10, 2007).

[vi] Vt. Stat. Ann. tit. 8, § 6004 (2006).

[vii] Ariz. Rev. Stat. Ann. § 20-1098.03 (2002).

[viii] S.D.Codified Laws § 58-46-8 (2007).

[ix] IRS Rev. Rul. 2005-40 (July 5, 2005).

[x] *Id.*

[xi] *Clougherty Packing Co. v. Commissioner*, 811 F.2d 1297, 1300 (9th Cir. 1987).

[xii] IRS Rev. Rul. 2005-40 (July 5, 2005).

[xiii] *Id.*

[xiv] I.R.C. § 501(c)(15)(A)(i).

[xv] I.R.C. § 162; Rev. Rul. 2005-40 (July 5, 2005).

[xvi] http://www.vermontcaptive.com/basics/HowToStart.cfm (accessed September 14, 2007).

[xvii] http://www.ins.state.ny.us/website3/captives/capform.htm (accessed September 14, 2007).

[xviii] *Captive Insurance Company Feasibility Study.* http://www.captive.utah.gov/docs/Feasibility_Study_Out line.doc (accessed October 17, 2007).

[xix] *ICCIE Designation Program.* http://www.iccie.org/ programs/ (accessed December 10, 2007).

[xx] Vt. Captive Fin. Reg. 81-2 § 3 (1999).